Excel 2000
fast&easy™

Send Us Your Comments

To comment on this book or any other PRIMA TECH title, visit our reader response page on the Web at **www.prima-tech.com/comments**.

How to Order

For information on quantity discounts, contact the publisher: Prima Publishing, P.O. Box 1260BK, Rocklin, CA 95677-1260; (916) 632-4400. On your letterhead, include information concerning the intended use of the books and the number of books you wish to purchase. For individual orders, visit PRIMA TECH's Web site at **www.prima-tech.com**.

Excel 2000

fast&easy™

Faithe Wempen

A DIVISION OF PRIMA PUBLISHING

A Division of Prima Publishing

Prima Publishing and colophon are registered trademarks of Prima Communications, Inc. PRIMA TECH and Fast & Easy are trademarks of Prima Communications, Inc., Rocklin, California 95677.

Publisher: Stacy L. Hiquet
Associate Publisher: Nancy Stevenson
Managing Editor: Dan J. Foster
Senior Acquisitions Editor: Deborah F. Abshier
Senior Editor: Kelli R. Crump
Project Editor: Geneil Breeze
Technical Reviewer: Ray Link
Interior Layout: Marian Hartsough
Cover Design: Prima Design Team
Indexer: Katherine Stimson

Microsoft, Windows, Windows NT, Outlook, PowerPoint, PhotoDraw, MSN, and FrontPage are trademarks or registered trademarks of Microsoft Corporation.

Important: If you have problems installing or running Microsoft Excel, go to Microsoft's Web site at **www.microsoft.com**. Prima Publishing cannot provide software support.

ISBN: 0-7615-1761-8
Library of Congress Catalog Card Number: 98-68145
Printed in the United States of America

02 03 DD 10 9 8 7 6 5 4 3 2

To Margaret

Acknowledgments

Thanks once again to a great team at Prima for another good editorial experience. Geneil Breeze, Project Editor, managed the whole thing seamlessly from start to finish. Debbie Abshier, the best acquisitions editor in the business (ask anyone!), made the contractual and legal parts go painlessly. This book was truly a team effort.

About the Author

FAITHE WEMPEN owns and operates Your Computer Friend, a computer training and troubleshooting business in Indianapolis that specializes in helping individuals and small businesses with their PCs. She is also an A+ Certified computer technician with advanced training in computer hardware troubleshooting and repair. Faithe has an M.A. in English from Purdue University, where her area of specialty was Rhetoric and Composition. Her eclectic writing credits include more than 30 computer books, including *Upgrade Your PC in a Weekend* and *The Essential Excel 2000 Book*, as well as training manuals, OEM documentation, and magazine articles.

Contents at a Glance

Contents

Introduction

This new *Fast & Easy* guide from Prima Publishing will help you open up the power of Microsoft Excel, the world's best-selling worksheet program. Worksheet—or spreadsheet—software is designed to organize numerical data into rows and columns on your computer screen. These types of programs have revolutionized the way that we work with numbers and have made even the most complex and challenging computations accessible to everyday people like you.

With many worksheet programs, new users can easily get lost in a maze of grids and formulas, and the result of a hard day's work usually ends up being frustration. *Fast & Easy* guides teach you with a step-by-step approach, clear language, and illustrations of exactly what you will see on your screen. *Excel 2000 Fast & Easy* provides the tools you need to successfully tackle the potentially overwhelming challenge of learning to use Excel 2000. You will be able to quickly tap into the program's user-friendly design and powerful worksheet calculating capability.

Who Should Read This Book?

The easy-to-follow, highly visual nature of this book makes it the perfect learning tool for a beginning computer user. It is also ideal, however, for those who are new to this version of Excel, or those who feel comfortable with computers and software, but have never used a spreadsheet program before.

In addition, anyone using a software application always needs an occasional reminder about the steps required to perform a particular task. By using *Excel 2000 Fast & Easy*, any level of user can look up steps for a task quickly without having to plow through pages of descriptions. In short, this book can be used by the beginning-to-intermediate computer user as a learning tool or as a step-by-step task reference.

Added Advice to Make You a Pro

This book uses steps and keeps explanations to a minimum to help you learn faster. Included in the book are a few elements that provide some additional comments to help you master the program, without encumbering your progress through the steps:

- **Tips** offer shortcuts when performing an action, or hints about features that might make your work in Excel quicker and easier.

- **Notes** give you a bit of background or additional information about a feature, or advice about how to use the feature in your day-to-day activities.

Read and enjoy this *Fast & Easy* book. It is certainly the fastest and easiest way to learn Microsoft Excel 2000!

PART I
Building Your First Worksheet

1

Welcome to Excel 2000

Excel is a replacement for the accountant's columnar pad, sharp pencil, and calculator. However, you don't have to be an accountant to benefit from Excel. If you have complex calculations to figure out, Excel can handle them with ease. Yet even if your calculations are simple, Excel will make working with numbers fun and easy. The great thing about Excel is that you can present your data so that it has impact. You can create colorful charts, print transparencies or hard copy reports, add clip art and your company logo, and more! In this chapter, you'll learn how to:

- Start Excel 2000
- Enter text and numbers
- Enter a simple formula
- Play "what if?"
- Close a worksheet

Starting Excel 2000

The Windows Start button is the easiest way to find your programs.

1. **Click** on the **Start button** on the Taskbar with the left mouse button. A pop-up menu will appear.

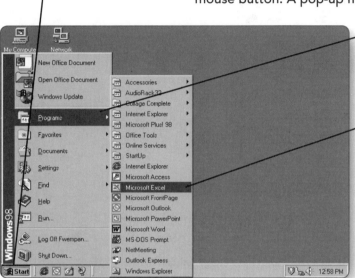

2. **Move** the **mouse arrow** up the menu to **Programs** to highlight it. A second pop-up menu will appear.

3. **Move** the **mouse arrow** to the right and **click** on **Microsoft Excel**. An Excel 2000 splash screen will appear briefly before the main Excel window opens.

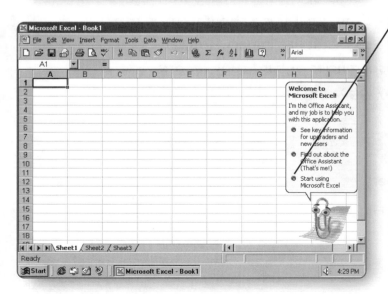

NOTE

If the Office Assistant appears, ignore him for now. The first time you start Excel, a balloon may appear over his head welcoming you to Excel. If you see that, click on the blue button next to Start using Microsoft Excel to make it go away. For more information about working with Office Assistant, see the "Getting Help" section in Chapter 2, "What's on the Excel Screen?"

Entering Text and Numbers

A *spreadsheet* is a rectangular grid of rows and columns. The columns are labeled with letters and the rows with numbers. The intersection of a row and a column is a *cell*. Each cell has an address, which is the column letter followed by the row number. For example, cell C10 is at the intersection of column C and row 10.

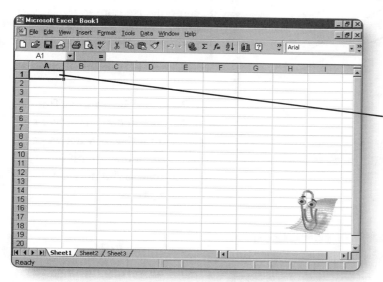

When you first open Excel, you'll notice that cell A1 has a border around it. This is the *active cell*.

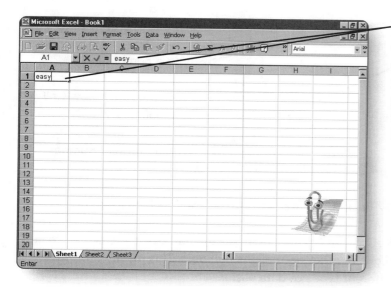

1. **Type text** in the active cell. A flashing insertion point will appear at the end of whatever you type. You'll notice that what you type will appear not only in the active cell but also in the Formula bar.

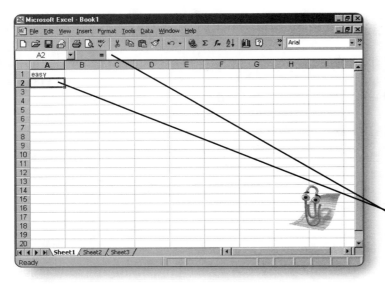

NOTE

Text entries are called *labels*. Labels may contain any combination of letters, numbers, or symbols. Excel can only use numeric entries or values in a calculation. It cannot use labels.

2. Press the **Enter key**. The cell below the current active cell will become the new active cell. The Formula bar will be empty again because the new active cell is empty.

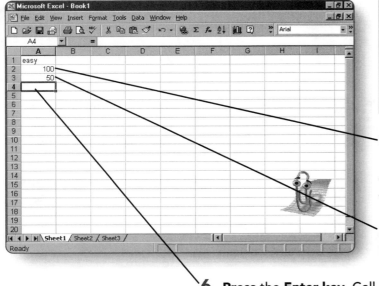

TIP

Another way to make a different cell active is to use the arrow keys on your keyboard.

3. Type a number in A2.

4. Press the **Enter key**. Cell A3 will be highlighted.

5. Type a different number in A3.

6. Press the **Enter key**. Cell A4 will be highlighted.

Notice that Excel right aligns the number in the cell. Excel left aligns *text* but right aligns *numbers*. This makes viewing different types of data easier.

Entering a Formula

In this section, you create a simple formula in a single cell, which adds two numbers together. First, make sure that the active cell is empty and located where you want the result of the formula to appear.

1. Type **=** (the equal sign) in **cell A4**.

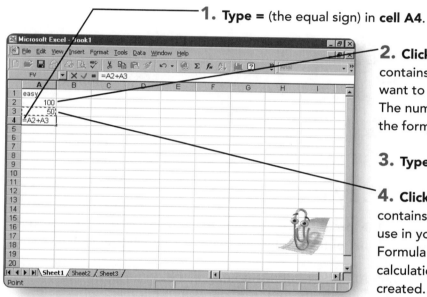

2. **Click** on **cell A2**, which contains the first number you want to use in the calculation. The number will be added to the formula in A4.

3. Type **+** (the plus sign).

4. **Click** on **cell A3**, which contains the second number to use in your formula. In the Formula bar, you will see the calculation that has been created.

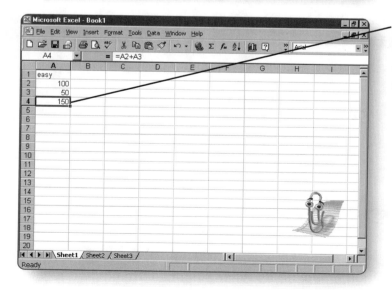

5. **Press** the **Enter key**. The formula will perform the calculation, and the result will appear in the active cell.

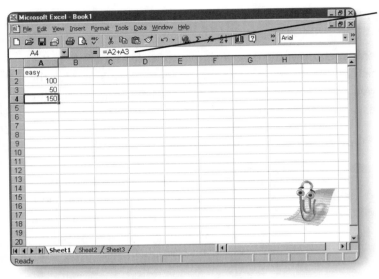

If you move the pointer back up to the cell where the answer appears, you can see that the cell contains the result, but if you look at the Formula bar, you can see that it still displays the formula you created.

Playing "What If?"

The formula remains stored in the cell so that you can change either of the numbers used in the calculation at any time.

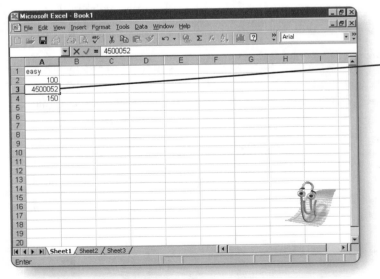

1. Click on **cell A3**. The cell will be highlighted.

2. Type a **different number**. The number will appear in the cell.

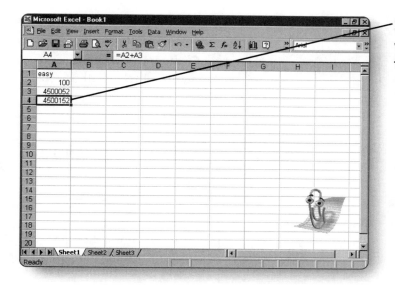

3. Press the **Enter key**. Excel will automatically recalculate the total in A4.

Excel can perform the calculation because it not only displays the result in the cell, but it also stores the formula. The formula isn't 100 + 50, which is how you calculate on a calculator, but A2 + A3, which still appears in the Formula bar.

This is one of the main reasons why Excel is so powerful. After you've set up a relationship between cells in a formula, you can change any of the numbers in those cells, but the relationship in the formula remains.

Closing a Worksheet

Now you are ready to close the worksheet. You can choose to save changes made to this worksheet so that they are available the next time you open it, or you can close the worksheet without saving any changes.

1. **Click** on **File**. The File menu will appear.

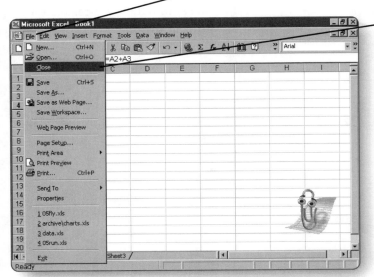

2. **Click** on **Close**. Office Assistant will ask whether you want to save the changes to Book1.

3. **Click** on **No**. Your changes will not be saved.

TIP

For more information on closing worksheets and exiting Excel, turn to Chapter 3, "Saving, Printing, and Exiting Excel."

2

What's on the Excel Screen?

A multitude of buttons and icons appears in the Excel window. Some icons make it easy to guess what the button does; however, some are less obvious. Learning to use all the elements of the Excel screen is an important part of using Excel. In this chapter, you'll learn how to:

- ● Select menu commands
- ● Use toolbars
- ● Work with dialog boxes
- ● Get help when you need it

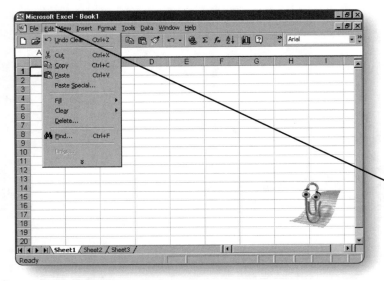

Using Menus

Menus are lists of commands, options, and other program features that you can activate. For example, you can choose a menu command to underline text or save your work.

1. Click on the **name of the menu** that you want to open. The menu will appear.

2. Pause a moment, or **click again** on the menu name. The complete list of menu items will appear.

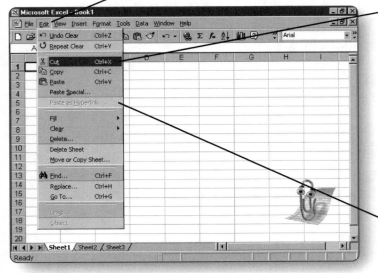

3a. Click on a **command**. A specific action will be performed, or a dialog box will open.

OR

3b. Move the **mouse pointer** away from the menu and **click**. The menu will close without issuing a command.

A dimmed command is not available at the moment.

NOTE

If you want Excel to show the complete menu immediately, without your having to pause in step 2, see "Changing How Menus and Toolbars Work" later in this chapter.

Understanding Menu Items

Excel's menus contain various items that give you at-a-glance information about a menu's commands.

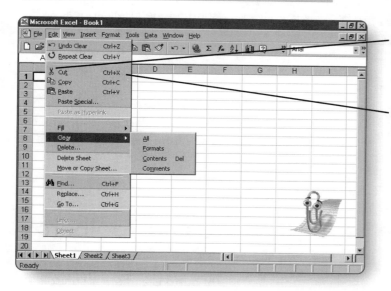

A picture indicates that there is a toolbar equivalent for the command.

Keyboard shortcuts, alternatives to using the menu command, are listed when available.

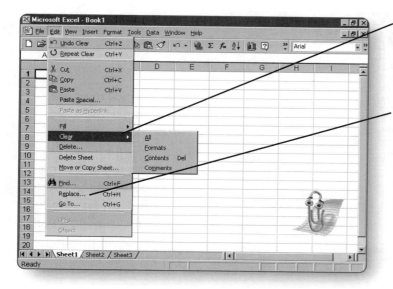

A right-pointing arrow indicates that a submenu is available. Pointing to the command opens the submenu.

An ellipsis (...) next to a command indicates that a dialog box will open when you click on that command. See "Working with Dialog Boxes" later in this chapter.

Using Shortcut Menus

You can right-click on almost any cell or other object in Excel to open a context-sensitive shortcut menu. The menu contains commands applicable to that object.

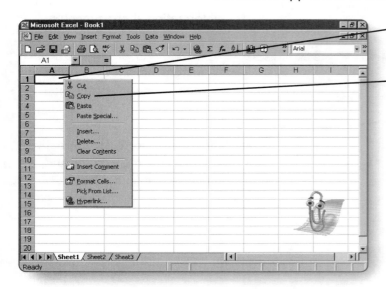

1. **Right-click** on a **cell**. A shortcut menu will appear.

2. **Click** (normally, with the left mouse button) on a **command**.

To close the menu without making a selection, click an area away from the menu.

Using Toolbars

Toolbars are organized groups of buttons and other controls that issue commands or apply formatting. They serve as alternatives to using the menu commands.

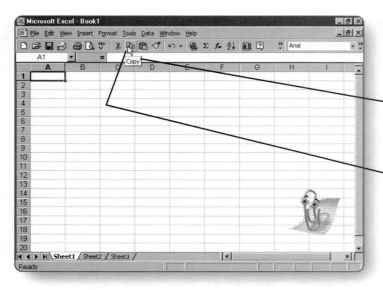

1. **Move** the **mouse arrow** over any button in the toolbar. The button name will appear.

2. **Click** on a **toolbar button**. Some controls on the toolbars employ drop-down lists, which are somewhat like menus. Such controls have down-pointing arrows (▼) to their right.

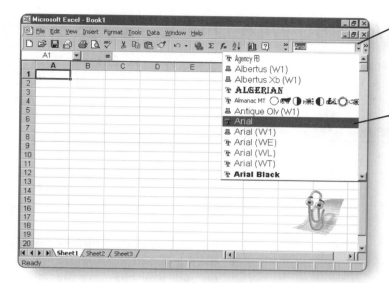

3. **Click** on a **down arrow (▼)** next to a button or other control. A drop-down list will appear.

4. **Click** on **your selection** from the list.

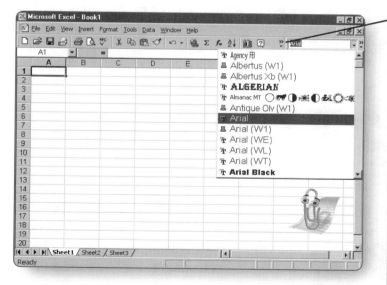

Because the Standard and Formatting toolbars share a row, some toolbar controls are not visible. To see them, click the >> button at the right end of the toolbar to open a drop-down list of additional controls.

NOTE

To place the Standard and Formatting toolbars on separate rows, so that all the tools are visible for each, see "Changing How Menus and Toolbars Work" later in this chapter.

Working with Dialog Boxes

Many menu commands are followed by three dots (an *ellipsis* . . .). This indicates that a dialog box opens when you select the command. Here's an example.

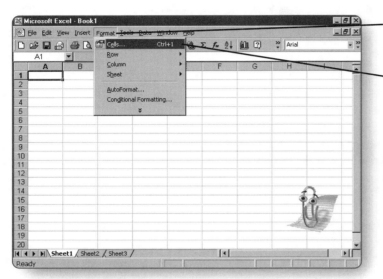

1. Click on **Format**. The Format menu will appear.

2. Click on **Cells**. The Format Cells dialog box will open.

Notice how related options have been grouped together on tabbed panels to make things easier to find. You can select from the groups Number, Alignment, Font, Border, Patterns, and Protection.

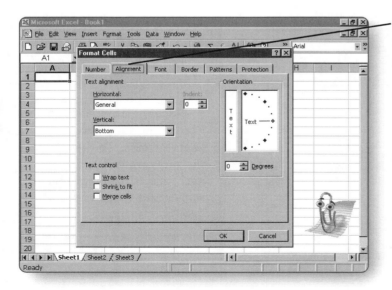

3. Click on the **Alignment tab**. The Alignment options will appear.

- Select from drop-down lists by clicking on a down arrow (▼).

- Turn features on or off by clicking on a box to insert or remove a ✔.

- Adjust numbers in dialog boxes by clicking on up and down arrows like these (♦).

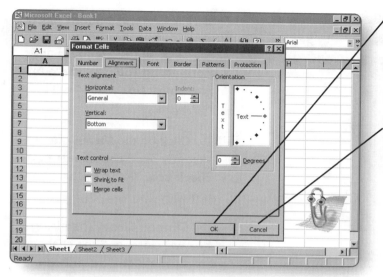

4a. **Click** on **OK**. Selections made in the dialog box will be implemented.

OR

4b. **Click** on **Cancel**. The dialog box will close, and no changes will be made.

Changing How Menus and Toolbars Work

Some people do not like Excel 2000's new menu and toolbar features. You might prefer that the menus show a full list of commands immediately or that the Standard and Formatting toolbars appear on separate rows.

1. **Click** on **Tools**. The Tools menu will appear.

2. **Click** on **Customize**. The Customize dialog box will open.

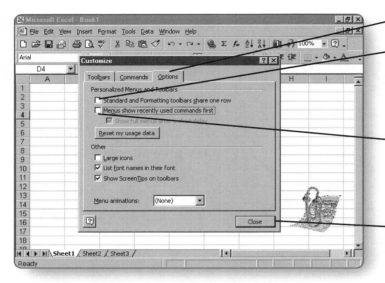

3. Click on the **Options** tab.

4. **Click** on the **Standard and Formatting toolbars share one row check box**. The ✔ will be removed.

5. **Click** on the **Menus show recently used commands first check box**. The ✔ will be removed.

6. **Click** on **Close**. The dialog box will close, and the changes will take effect.

NOTE

In the rest of this book, the figures will show both of these features turned off, just as you turned them off in the preceding steps.

Moving Around the Screen with Scroll Bars

You can move around an Excel worksheet in several ways.

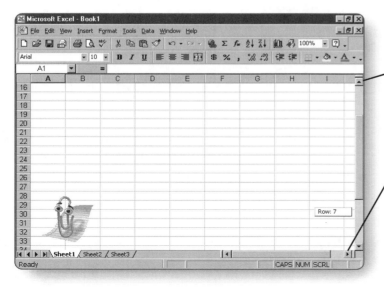

1. **Click repeatedly** on the **arrow** at either end of the vertical scroll bar. The worksheet will move up or down in the window.

2. **Click repeatedly** on the **arrow** at either end of the horizontal scroll bar. The worksheet will move left or right.

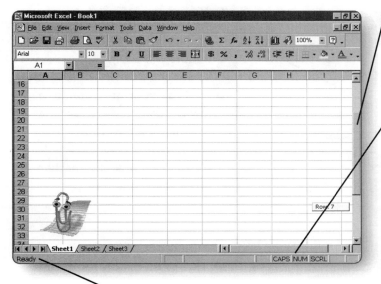

3. Hold the **mouse button** and **drag** the **vertical scroll box** up or down. An indicator box will appear telling you which row you're scrolling over.

At the right end of the status bar is an indicator area that shows whether the CAPS lock, the NUM lock for the numbers keypad, or the Scroll lock are activated. If they are, an abbreviation appears in one of these boxes; if they aren't active, the blocks are empty. In this screen, all three locks, CAPS, NUM, and SCRL, are activated.

Below the horizontal scroll bar is the status bar, which tells you about operations in progress in Excel. Most of the time, the status bar reads "Ready." When this setting is showing, you can work with the worksheet.

Getting Help from Office Assistant

When you opened Excel 2000 for the first time, you probably noticed that cute animated paper clip trying to get your attention. That's the Office Assistant, Excel's main Help tool.

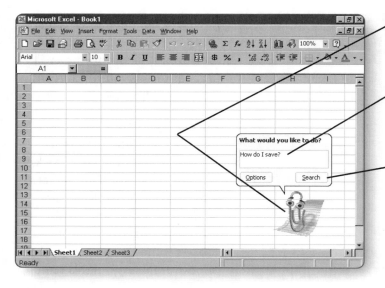

1. **Click** on the **Office Assistant**. The Office Assistant's bubble will open.

2. **Type your question**, or a few words that describe what you need help with.

3. **Click** on **Search**. Another window will open.

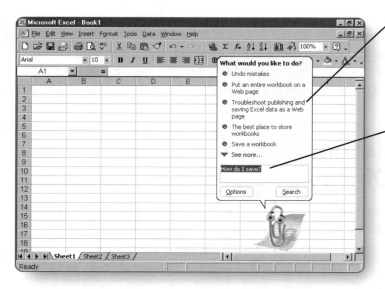

4. **Click** on the **topic button** representing the subject you need help with. The topic will appear in the Microsoft Excel Help window.

You could also type in a different question and click Search again, or click See more if none of the topics is useful.

NOTE

Frequently, Office Assistant opens simply because you've performed particular keystrokes. In this situation, Office Assistant immediately offers you context-sensitive help—options it thinks are related to the task you're performing.

5. **Read** the **Help information** that appears. Do any of the following:

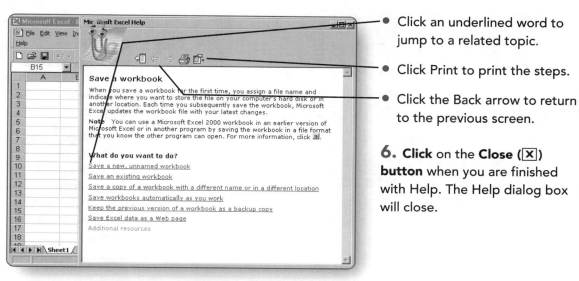

- Click an underlined word to jump to a related topic.

- Click Print to print the steps.

- Click the Back arrow to return to the previous screen.

6. **Click** on the **Close ([X])** **button** when you are finished with Help. The Help dialog box will close.

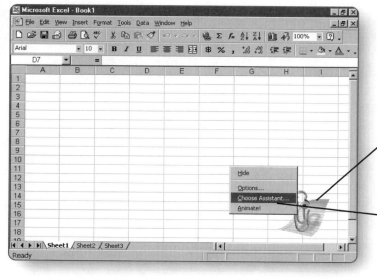

Changing the Office Assistant

You can choose a different character to be your helper if you don't like the paper clip.

1. **Right-click** on the **Office Assistant**. A shortcut menu will appear.

2. **Click** on **Choose Assistant**. The Office Assistant dialog box will open.

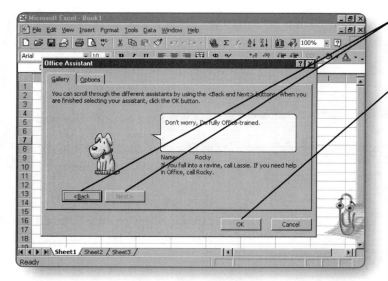

3. Click on the **Next** and **Back buttons**. The available assistants will appear.

4. Click on **OK** when an assistant appears that you like.

NOTE

If you see a message that the selected assistant is not installed, click on Yes and insert your Office 2000 (or Excel 2000) CD so that the new assistant can be installed.

3

Saving, Printing, and Exiting Excel

Everyone who uses a computer has probably lost data at one time or another. If you haven't been saving to a disk regularly, remember that it only takes a few seconds to lose hours of work. You'll also probably want to make printouts of your work to share with others. You could use the hard copy as a report or possibly on a transparency as part of a presentation. In this chapter, you'll learn how to:

- Save a worksheet
- Print your document
- Exit Excel

Save, Save, and Save Again!

Computer users know they must save their work, but many forget, until something important is lost. Not only is it important to save your work so that you don't have to redo it, but saving also gives you the opportunity to file your work electronically, so that you know where to find it.

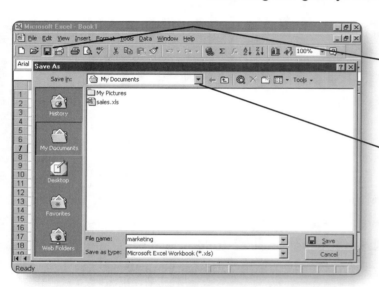

1. Click on the **Save button**. If this is the first time you've saved the document, the Save As dialog box will open.

Save in: offers you a folder where you can save your worksheet. If you haven't made any changes to your software, the default folder that appears is the My Documents folder. If you want to select a different disk or folder, click on the down arrow (▼).

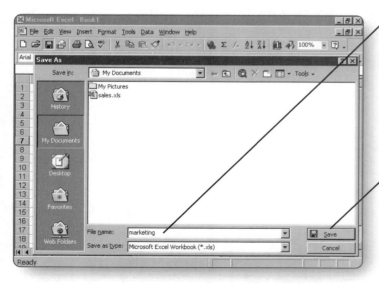

2. Type a **name** for your file in the File name: text box. Excel will offer you "Book1" as a name. It's not a good idea to accept this because by the time you get to "Book9," it's going to be difficult to remember what exactly you saved in Book3 or 4.

3. Click on **Save**. Your document will be stored on a disk. Excel automatically adds an .xls extension to the filename. This indicates the file format used to save Excel files.

TIP

If you want to save a copy of your file with a different name, click on File and Save As to open the Save As dialog box again.

4. **Click** on the **Save button** regularly, to continue to save your document as you work on it. The Save As dialog box will not open again.

Printing a Document

Whether you need to share a budget report with your colleagues or your retirement savings projection with your spouse, you need to print your file on paper.

Printing with the Print Button

If you just need one copy of the worksheet you currently are working on, the fastest and easiest way to print is to use the Print button on the Standard toolbar.

1. **Click** on the **Print button**. One copy of everything on the current worksheet will be immediately sent to the printer.

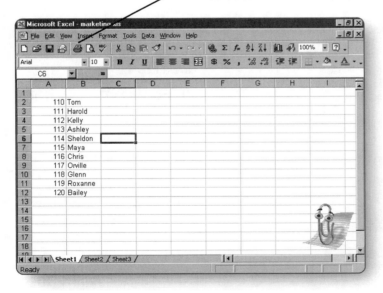

Printing with the Print Dialog Box

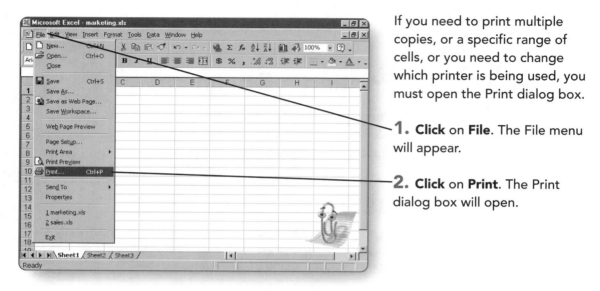

If you need to print multiple copies, or a specific range of cells, or you need to change which printer is being used, you must open the Print dialog box.

1. Click on **File**. The File menu will appear.

2. Click on **Print**. The Print dialog box will open.

3. Set any of the following **options**:

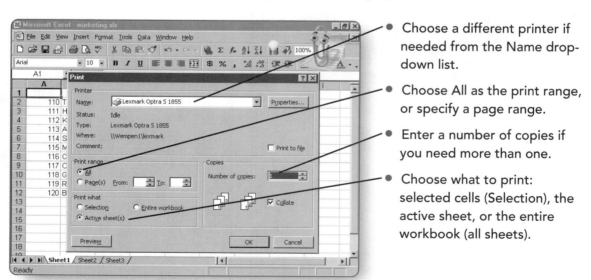

- Choose a different printer if needed from the Name drop-down list.

- Choose All as the print range, or specify a page range.

- Enter a number of copies if you need more than one.

- Choose what to print: selected cells (Selection), the active sheet, or the entire workbook (all sheets).

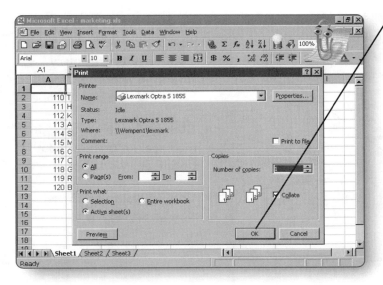

4. Click on **OK** when you've made your selections. The pages will be sent to the printer.

NOTE

If you do not want the entire worksheet or workbook printed, select the range of cells you want to print before performing these steps. See Chapter 5, "Editing Worksheets," to learn about selecting cells.

Exiting Excel

You can exit Excel in several ways. This section shows you how to exit by using the menu bar.

1. Click on **File**. The File menu will appear.

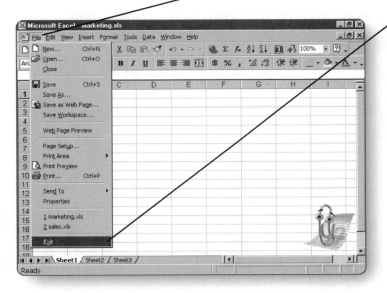

2. Click on **Exit**. The Excel program will close.

If an open workbook hasn't been saved, the Office Assistant asks whether you want to save changes to that particular file. (If you have hidden the Office Assistant, a dialog box asks the same question.)

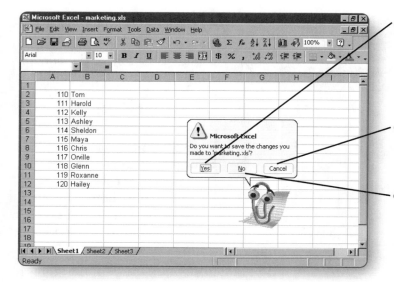

● Click on Yes, to save the workbook specified and exit. If you haven't previously saved the workbook, the Save As dialog box will open.

● Click on Cancel to return to the Excel program without closing any workbooks.

● Click on No, to exit Excel without saving any changes.

NOTE

If you have more than one workbook open with unsaved changes, the Office Assistant's message (or the dialog box) also includes a Yes to All option. Choosing this is the same as choosing Yes for each workbook individually.

4

Managing Workbooks and Worksheets

A *workbook* is an electronic file that contains one or more worksheets. The *worksheets* are like pages of a book that are available to you when your book (workbook) is open. Just as you can have different folders or books piled on the top of your desk at one time, you can have more than one workbook open at a time in Excel. You can easily switch between workbooks and worksheets as well. In this chapter, you'll learn how to:

- Create a new workbook
- Open and close workbooks
- View multiple workbooks
- Add, name, and delete worksheets

Creating a New Workbook

Before you can learn to manage workbooks and worksheets, you must know how to create a new workbook.

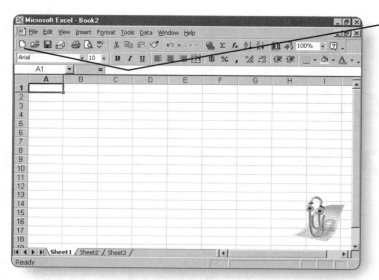

1. **Click** on the **New button**. A new worksheet will open with the title "Book2," but your title could be different because it reflects how many workbooks you've created during this session.

TIP

Don't forget to save your workbook soon. You don't want to lose any work you've done!

Moving Between Workbooks

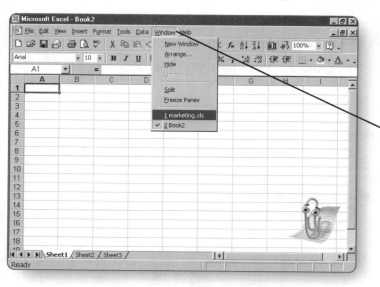

Often your work requires you to work with multiple workbooks. Excel enables you to move easily between more than one workbook.

1. **Click** on **Window**. The Window menu will appear.

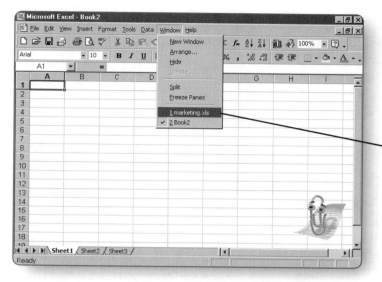

At the bottom of the Window menu is a list of the files you have open. The file with the ✔ next to it is the file that you are currently working on in the main Excel window.

2. Click on the **filename** of the file you want to work with. The file you specify will be displayed onscreen.

Viewing Multiple Workbooks

In Excel, you can have more than one workbook open and view more than one workbook onscreen at a time. You can also view workbooks tiled on the screen with the screen divided into multiple windows, one for each workbook.

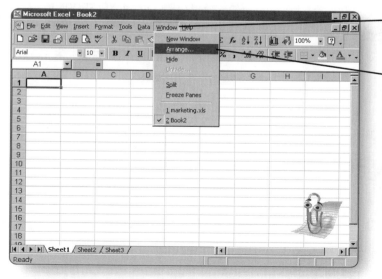

1. Click on **Window**. The Window menu will appear.

2. Click on **Arrange**. The Arrange Windows dialog box will open. It will ask you whether you want to tile the workbooks, show all the workbooks vertically or horizontally across the screen, or cascade one title bar under the next.

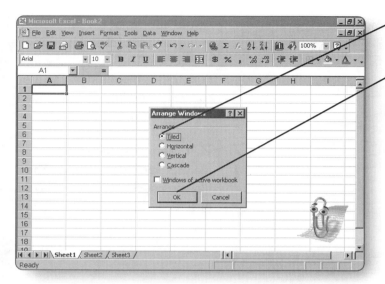

3. **Click** on **Tiled**. The item will be selected.

4. **Click** on **OK**. The workbooks will be tiled onscreen.

You can work in any of the workbooks by clicking in it, to make it active. Use the scroll bar to move quickly through the worksheet data.

To maximize one workbook, so that it fills the entire work area, click twice (double-click) on the title bar for that workbook.

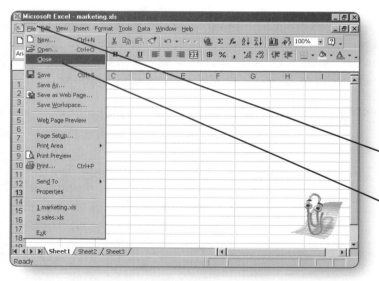

Closing a Workbook

As with closing Excel, one easy way to close a workbook is to use the File menu.

1. **Click** on **File**. The File menu will appear.

2. **Click** on **Close**. Office Assistant will appear and ask whether you want to save changes.

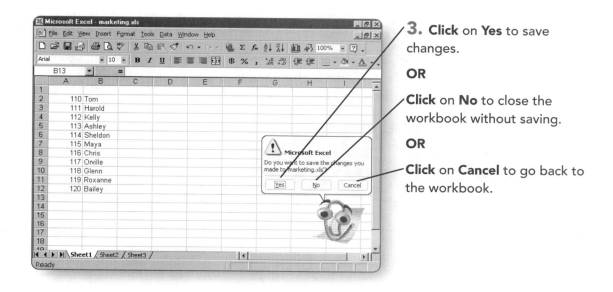

3. Click on **Yes** to save changes.

OR

Click on **No** to close the workbook without saving.

OR

Click on **Cancel** to go back to the workbook.

Opening an Existing Workbook

You can open an existing workbook (a workbook that has previously been saved on a disk) in two ways. If you've been working on the workbook recently, it probably will still be listed at the bottom of the File menu. If it's not listed, you'll need to search for its location on a disk.

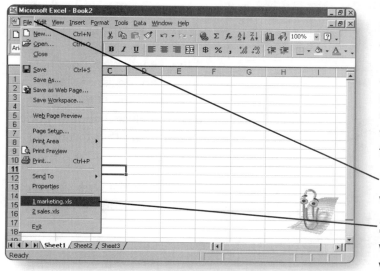

Opening with the File Menu

As you might expect, Excel gives you more than one way to open a workbook. Opening a workbook with the File menu is fast and easy.

1. Click on **File**. The File menu will appear.

2. Click on the **worksheet** you want to work on. The worksheet will appear onscreen.

Opening with the Open Button

If you prefer to use the toolbar rather than the menu, you can use the Open button to open a workbook just as easily as with the File menu.

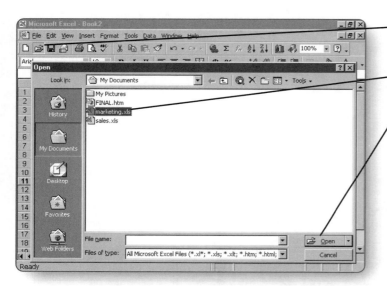

1. **Click** on the **Open button**. The Open dialog box will appear.

2. **Click** on the **file** you want to open. The file will be highlighted.

3. **Click** on **Open**. The selected file will appear onscreen.

NOTE

If the file you want is not in the default folder (C:\My Documents), see the procedure in the following section.

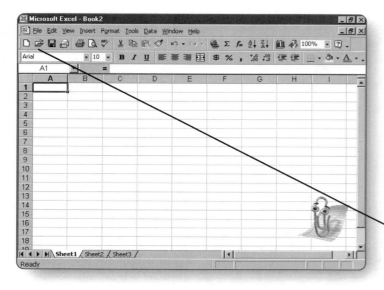

Opening a File from Another Location

If the file you want does not appear on the list of files shown by default in the Open dialog box, you must change the drive and/or folder that this dialog box shows.

1. **Click** on the **Open button**. The Open dialog box will appear.

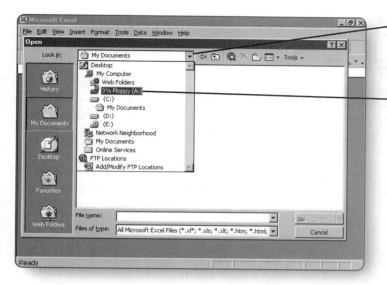

2. **Click** the **down arrow (▼)** next to the Look in: box. The drop-down list will appear.

3. **Click** on the **drive** that contains the file. The drive's contents will appear.

Some drives contain multiple folders. If the file is stored in a folder, you will need to navigate into that folder. If the drive does not contain folders (a floppy disk might not, for example), you can skip step 4.

4. If needed, **double-click** on the **folder** to move to. You may have to navigate through several layers of folders to find the file.

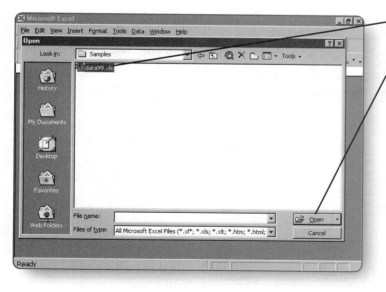

5. **Click** on the **file** you want to open. The file will be selected.

6. **Click** on **Open**. The file will open.

Working with Worksheets

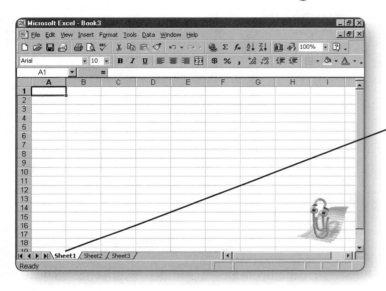

By default, each new workbook has three worksheets, and each worksheet has a Sheet tab, which you can see at the bottom of the workbook window.

1. Click on a **worksheet tab** to move to a different worksheet. The new worksheet will appear onscreen.

Naming a Worksheet

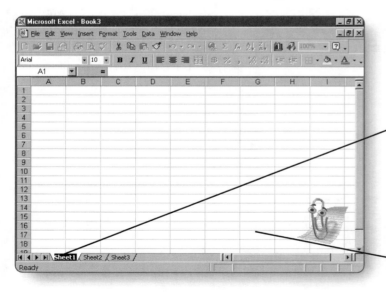

To organize and effectively manage your worksheets, give your worksheets names that remind you of what information they contain.

1. Double-click on the **tab** for the sheet you want to name. The current name will be highlighted and ready for editing.

2. Type a **new name**.

3. Click anywhere outside the tab. The name change will appear on the tab you selected.

Adding Worksheets to a Workbook

Excel gives you three worksheets for every workbook, but adding more worksheets is not a problem.

1. Click on **Insert**. The Insert menu will appear.

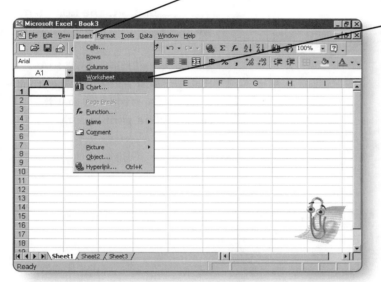

2. Click on **Worksheet**. A new worksheet will be added to your workbook.

NOTE

All the worksheets are saved each time you save the workbook.

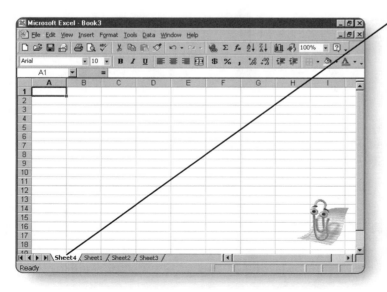

Notice that the new worksheet is added to the left of the worksheet that was active (on top) when you issued the command.

NOTE

You can rearrange the order of the tabs on the screen by clicking on one of the tabs and dragging it to a new location.

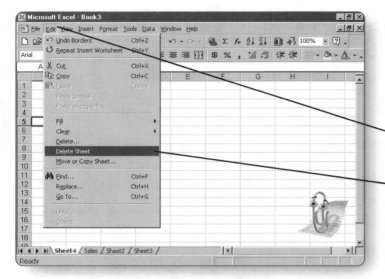

Deleting a Worksheet

If you no longer need a work-sheet, it's easy to get rid of it.

1. **Click** on **Edit**. The Edit menu will appear.

2. **Click** on **Delete Sheet**. A dialog box from Office Assistant will open and tell you that the sheet will be permanently deleted.

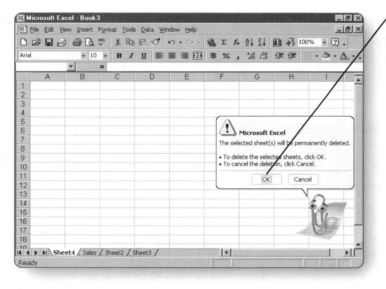

3. **Click** on **OK**. The worksheet will be deleted.

Part I Review Questions

1. What does a designation like C10 mean? *See "Entering Text and Numbers" in Chapter 1*

2. What are labels? *See "Entering Text and Numbers" in Chapter 1*

3. What happens to a cell that contains a formula when you change the number in a cell that it references? *See "Playing 'What If?'" in Chapter 1*

4. What does it mean when an ellipsis (. . .) appears after a menu command? *See "Understanding Menu Items" in Chapter 2*

5. How do you display a shortcut menu? *See "Using Shortcut Menus" in Chapter 2*

6. How can you save a copy of a file under a different name? *See "Save, Save, and Save Again!" in Chapter 3*

7. What happens when you click on the Print button? *See "Printing with the Print Button" in Chapter 3*

8. What is the difference between a workbook and a worksheet? *See the introduction in Chapter 4*

9. How can you switch between workbooks when you have more than one workbook open? *See "Moving Between Workbooks" in Chapter 4*

10. When you insert a new worksheet into a workbook, where does Excel insert the new worksheet? *See "Adding Worksheets to a Workbook" in Chapter 4*

PART II

Constructing Larger Worksheets

5

Editing Worksheets

When you create a worksheet, a lot of data entry is involved. Excel has features to cut down on at least some of that repetitive work. Unfortunately, you'll still make mistakes, so you need to know how to edit cell entries and run spell-check. You'll probably also want to make some changes to the way you construct your worksheet. Some great features in Excel allow you to reorganize your worksheet without having to re-enter any data. In this chapter, you'll learn how to:

- Select and edit cells
- Delete data, rows, and columns
- Copy and move data
- Fill and transpose ranges
- Adjust column width and row height
- Spell-check a worksheet

Selecting Cells

Before you can work with many of the features in Excel, you need to know how to select cells. You can select a rectangular group of cells, called a *range*, in any of the following ways:

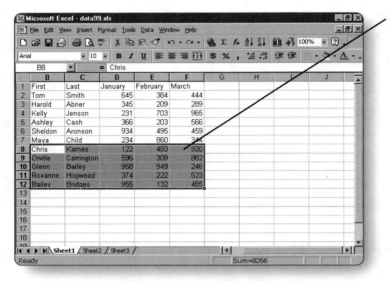

- Click and drag over the selection.

- Click in one cell, and then hold down the Shift key and click in the opposite corner of the selection.

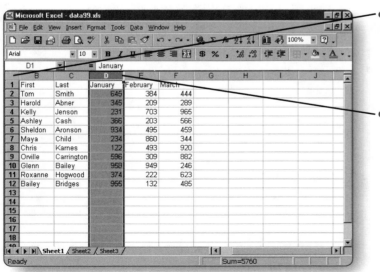

- Click on the Select All button, the gray rectangle where the column and row headings meet, to select the entire worksheet.

- Click in a column or row heading to select the whole column or row.

Editing Cell Content

When you enter new information in the Formula bar, you can edit it before you press the Enter key. You can delete characters using the Backspace key. You can also move the insertion point with the arrow keys and either insert text by typing or delete text by pressing the Delete or Backspace keys.

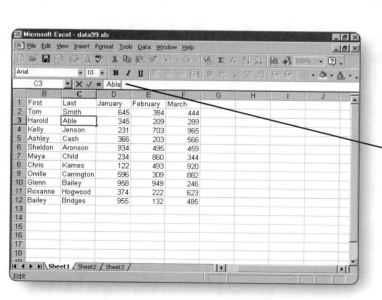

1. **Click** on a **cell**. The cell will be highlighted.

2. **Click** in the **Formula bar** to place the insertion point in the entry. You will now be able to insert or delete text.

3. **Press** the **right** or **left arrow key** to move the insertion point where you need to make a change.

4. **Press** the **Backspace key** to delete the character to the left of the insertion point, or **press** the **Delete key** to delete the character to the right.

5. **Type** new **text** as needed. The text will appear in the Formula bar and the selected cell.

6. **Press** the **Enter key**. The change will be accepted.

Replacing Cell Content

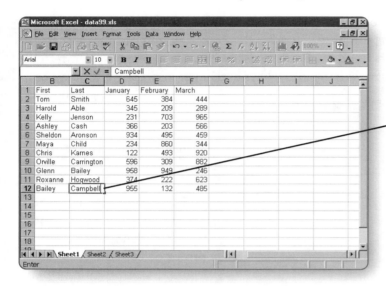

You can completely replace the content of a cell, rather than edit it.

1. Click on a **cell**.

2. Type the **new content**. Whatever you type will replace the old content.

3. Press the **Enter key**. The change will be accepted.

Removing Cell Content

You can remove all content from a single cell or a range of cells, leaving the cell or cells blank.

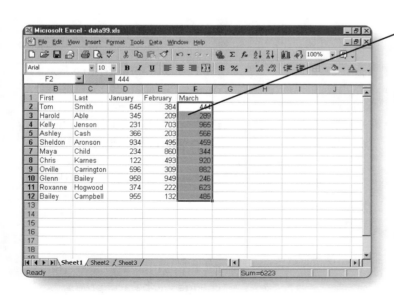

1. Select the **cell** or **range of cells** to clear.

2. Press the **Delete key**. The cells will be cleared.

NOTE

This procedure clears the content from the cell but leaves the empty cell in place. To remove the cell, so that surrounding content shifts, use the Delete command on the Edit menu.

Adding Rows and Columns

As you construct your worksheet, you'll occasionally find that you need to add rows and columns. To add a new row, you first select the row that the new one should appear above. Or, to add a new column, you select the column that the new one should appear to the left of.

1. **Click** in a **row** or **column head** to select it. The row or column you choose will be highlighted.

2. **Click** on **Insert**. The Insert menu will appear.

3. **Click** on **Rows** or **Columns**. The new row or column will be inserted before the row or column you initially selected.

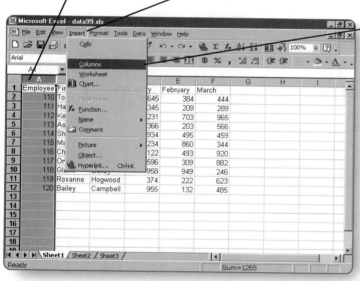

NOTE

Depending on whether you select a row or column, the menu item for a row or column will be either available or dimmed.

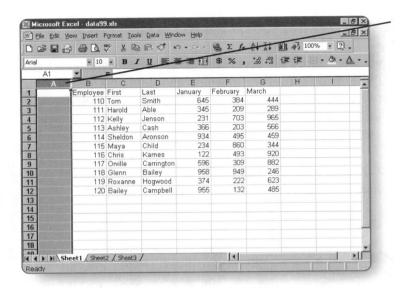

Notice that column A becomes column B, and a new column A is displayed.

Oops!—Using Undo and Redo

Sometimes you'll want to undo an action you've just completed in Excel.

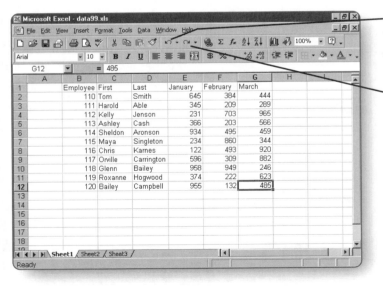

1. Click on the **Undo button**. The last action you performed will be undone.

If you make a mistake by undoing, immediately click the Redo button to get back what was undone.

Undoing Multiple Actions

After working in a worksheet for a while, there will be many levels of Undo that you can work back through.

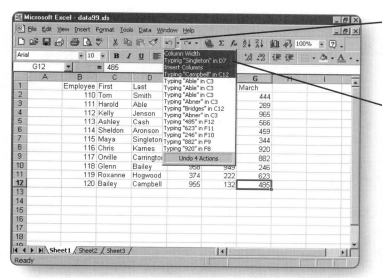

1. Click on the **down arrow** (▼) next to the Undo button. Your recent actions will be listed.

2. Click on the **action** you want to undo. That action and all actions you took after it will be undone.

NOTE

The Redo button also has a drop-down list, for multiple-action redoing.

Moving Data

One advantage of using Excel is the ease with which you can move and copy data.

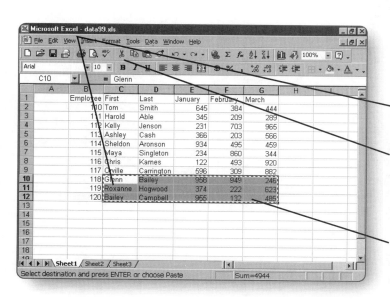

1. Select a **range of cells**. The cells will be highlighted.

2. Click on the **Cut button**. Moving dashes (called a *marquee*) will appear around your selection.

Notice that your data doesn't disappear like text does when cut in a word processor.

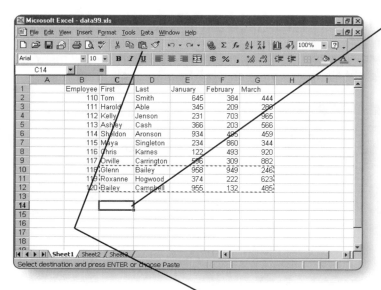

3. Click in the **cell** that will be the upper-left corner of the new location of the range. The cell will be selected.

NOTE

There must be enough empty cells in the new location to accommodate the cut data, or existing data will be overwritten.

4. Click on the **Paste button**. The data will be pasted in the new location.

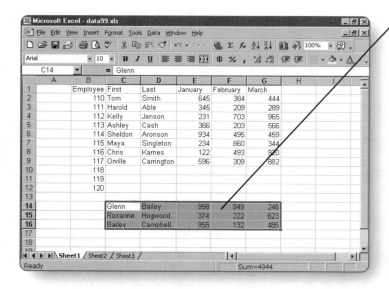

The pasted data will appear in the new location.

NOTE

Unlike in other Windows programs, in Excel after cutting and pasting, the selection does not remain on the Clipboard. If you want to paste additional copies of the selection, use the following procedure.

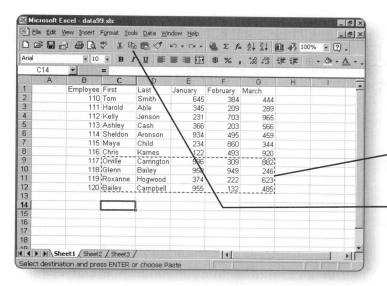

Copying Data

Copying places selected data in a new location. Unlike moved data, copied data also remains in the original location.

1. Select a **range of cells**. The cells will be highlighted.

2. Click on the **Copy button**. A marquee (running dashes) will appear around your selection.

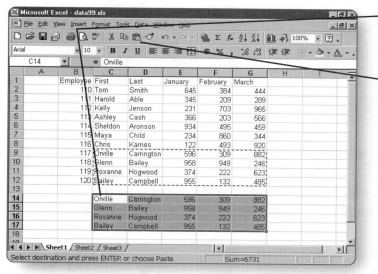

3. Click in the **cell** at the top left of the range where you want to place the copy.

4. Click on the **Paste button**. The selected range will appear in both the original location and the new location.

5. (Optional) **Repeat steps 3** and **4**. Another copy of the same selection will be pasted in a different spot.

6. Press the **Esc key** to turn off the marquee around the selection.

You can also use shortcut keys as a substitute for the Cut, Copy, and Paste buttons. To cut, press Ctrl+X; to copy, press Ctrl+C; and to paste, press Ctrl+V. Many experienced Excel users find these keyboard shortcuts more expedient than the toolbar buttons because they do not have to take their hand away from the keyboard to move the mouse.

Using Drag and Drop

A quick way to move or copy, if you're good with a mouse, is by using the Drag-and-Drop feature.

1. Select the **cells** you want to move or copy. The cells will be highlighted.

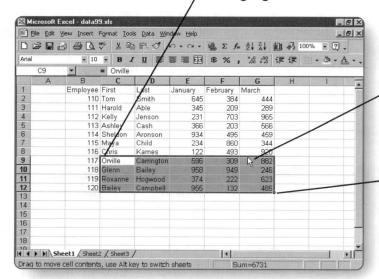

2. Hold down the **Ctrl key** if you want to copy. (To move, skip this step.)

3. Position the **mouse pointer** over the border of the selected area. The mouse pointer will become an arrow.

Avoid the lower-right corner of the range's border; this is the Fill handle and is used for a different purpose. See "Filling a Range" later in this chapter.

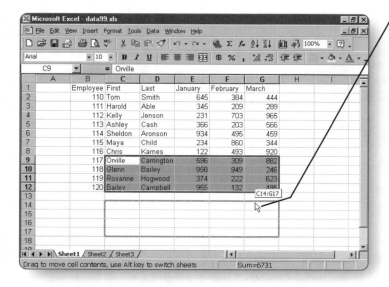

4. Press and **hold** the **mouse button** as you **drag** the cells to a new location. The cell location you're dragging over will appear in a box below the mouse arrow.

5. Release the **mouse button**. The cells will be dropped in the new location. This is much quicker than using buttons or menus!

Filling a Range

The Fill feature is for those who hate data entry. Excel can't do all the data entry for you, but it can do some of those repetitive tasks.

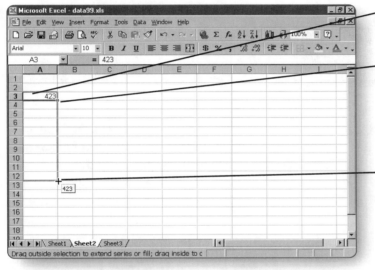

1. **Select** a **cell**. The cell will be highlighted.

2. **Click** on the **Fill handle** (the extra little square on the bottom-right corner of the highlighted cell). The mouse arrow will change to a plus sign.

3. **Press** and **hold** the **mouse button** and **drag** the **Fill handle** to the right or down a number of cells.

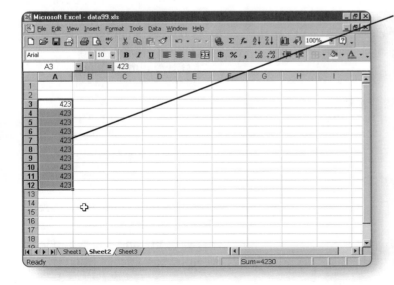

4. **Release** the **mouse button**. The original contents of the highlighted cell, whether it was a number or a formula, will be copied to all the cells you selected.

NOTE

Learn more about copying formulas in Chapter 6, "Using Formulas and Functions."

Filling with a Series

Not only can you fill a range with a number or formula, but you also can do it with a series. This is really how the Fill feature saves you time and effort. Suppose that you need to type the months of the year to construct a budget.

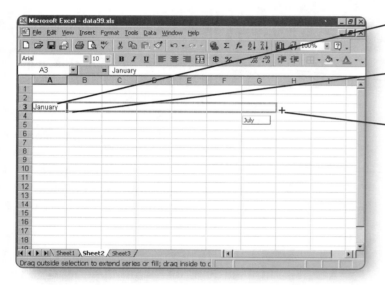

1. **Type** the **name** of a month in a cell.

2. **Click** on the **Fill handle** of that cell.

3. **Press** and **hold** the **mouse button** and **drag** the **Fill handle** to the right. You don't even need to count the cells because as you drag, Excel will show you exactly which month you're on!

NOTE

You can use this feature to fill month names, days of the week, or any series of numbers. To fill a series of numbers, enter the first two numbers in adjacent cells, so that Excel will know what interval you want. Then select those cells before dragging the Fill handle.

---

4. **Release** the **mouse button**. The months of the year following the one you typed in will be automatically inserted.

Transposing Cells

Imagine that you've entered five columns of data. Your fingers are aching from all that data entry, but now you realize that you don't really want the names in a row across the top of the worksheet. The worksheet would be much more effective and easier to work with, if the names were in a column. In this situation, you use the Transpose feature. The Transpose feature switches rows of cells to columns or columns to rows.

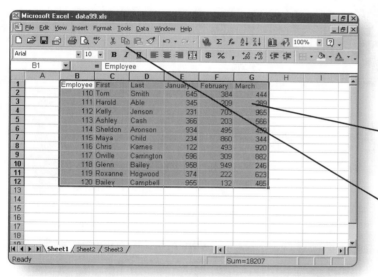

1. Select the **cells** you want to transpose. The cells will be highlighted.

2. Click on the **Copy button**. The cells you selected will be copied to the Clipboard.

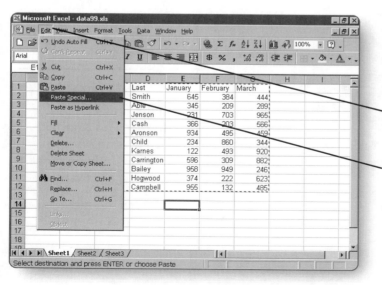

3. Click in the **cell** that will be the top-left corner of your new range. The cell will be highlighted.

4. Click on **Edit**. The Edit menu will appear.

5. Click on **Paste Special**. The Paste Special dialog box will open.

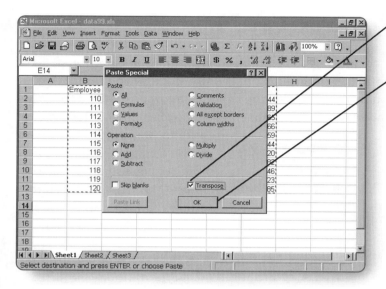

6. Click on **Transpose**. A ✔ will appear in the box.

7. Click on **OK**. The dialog box will close.

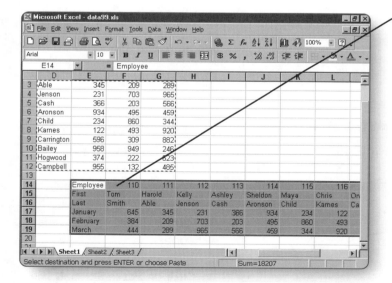

The entire table is displayed in the new location with rows converted to columns, and columns to rows.

8. Press the **Esc key**. The marquee around the original selection will be turned off.

NOTE

If you decide that transposing was a mistake, you can reverse it by clicking the Undo button immediately afterwards.

Adjusting Column Width and Row Height

When cell content is too long to fit in its cell, one of several things may happen:

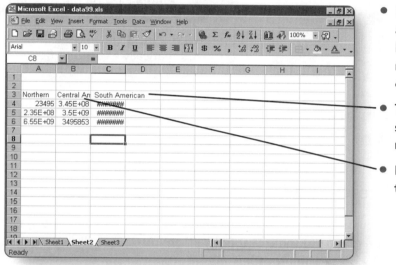

- Excel widens a column automatically as you enter long numbers (if you have not manually changed that column's width).

- Text labels that do not fit will spill into the next cell to the right if it is empty.

- If the next cell is not empty, text appears truncated.

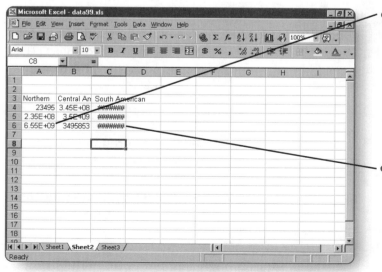

- If a plain number (not formatted with any special number formatting) will not fit and Excel cannot widen the column automatically, it appears in a shortened Scientific notation format if the column is wide enough to show it.

- If the column is too narrow to show the Scientific notation format of the number, or if the cell is formatted with a specific number format other than General, it appears as a series of # marks.

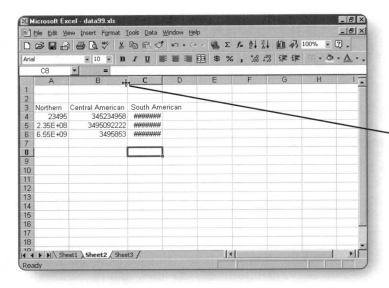

Resizing a Column to Fit

You can resize a column to fit its longest entry.

1. Double-click on the **dividing line** to the right of the column's letter. The column will automatically expand to fit the content.

Setting a Specific Column Width

You can manually widen a column (or make it more narrow) by dragging the same divider line that you double-clicked on in the preceding procedure.

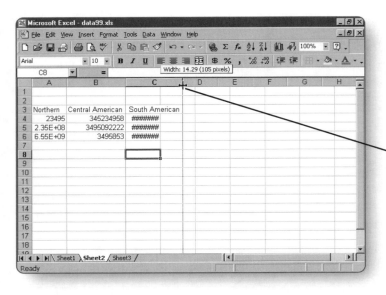

1. Move the **mouse arrow** to the divider between the column headings on the right side of the column you want to adjust. The mouse pointer will become a double-headed arrow.

2. Press and **hold** the **mouse button** and **drag** the **line** to resize the width of the column.

3. Release the **mouse button**. The changes will take effect.

There are other ways to change column width. Some are found on the Format, Column menu.

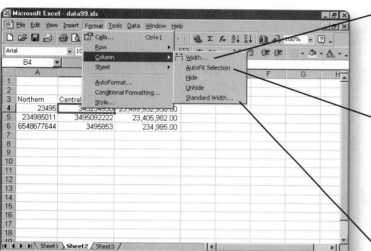

Use the Width command to open a dialog box in which you can enter a specific width, measured in characters of the default font (usually Arial 10-point).

AutoFit Selection is the same as double-clicking between the columns, except that it can apply to more than one column at a time if you select multiple columns first.

Standard Width changes the default width for columns on the worksheet.

Checking Your Spelling

After you've entered all your data, you will probably want to print your worksheet to share it with others. Before you take that step, it's a good idea to check your spelling. Even if you always won the spelling bee at school, you probably make the occasional typing error, and the Spelling feature may catch it.

However, be aware that the Spelling feature doesn't catch all mistakes. If you've made a typing or spelling error, such as using "led" instead of "lead," because both words are in the dictionary, Spelling will not catch this as an error. Therefore, it is still very important to proofread your work.

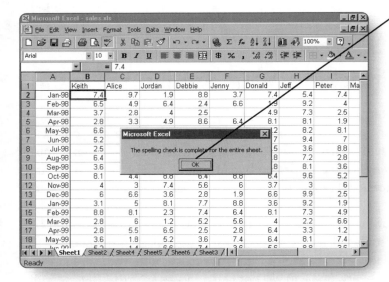

1. **Click** on the **Spelling button**. The Spelling dialog box will open.

If Excel doesn't find any errors, a dialog box will open that tells you the spell-check is complete. Click OK, and you're done. Otherwise, continue to step 2.

NOTE

The Spelling check searches from the active cell to the end of the worksheet. If the active cell was not A1 when you began the spelling check, then at some point during the spelling check, you will see a dialog box asking whether you want to continue checking at the beginning of the sheet. Click on Yes.

At the top of the dialog box next to Not in Dictionary:, Excel identifies the first item it can't match. Suggestions are listed with the first suggestion appearing in the Change to: text box.

2. Choose from the following **options**:

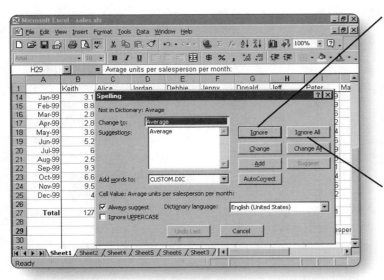

- **Ignore**. If the word highlighted is spelled correctly but is flagged because it does not appear in the dictionary (which often happens with proper names), click on this option to move to the next misspelling without making any changes.

- **Ignore All**. If the highlighted word is likely to continue to occur and is spelled correctly, click on this option to ignore all future occurrences.

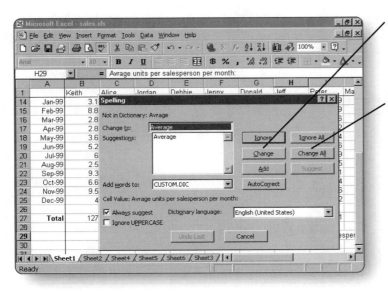

- **Change**. This option will change the misspelled word to the option displayed in the Change to: text box.

- **Change All**. This option will change this occurrence and all subsequent occurrences of the highlighted word to the option displayed in the Change to: text box.

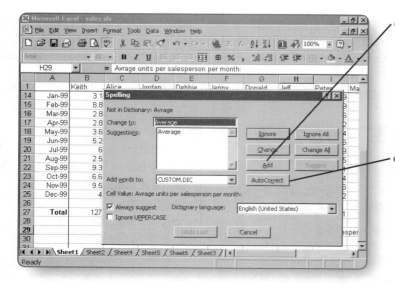

● **Add**. If the word is spelled correctly and you do not want Excel to continue to identify this word as a misspelling every time you run spell-check, click on Add to add the word to the dictionary.

● **AutoCorrect**. If a word you often misspell or mistype is identified, type the correct spelling in the Change to: text box. If you aren't sure of the spelling, click on Suggest, and then click on the correct spelling in the Suggestions: list. You can now add the misspelled word to the list of automatic corrections by clicking on AutoCorrect. Now as you enter the word in your worksheet, it will be automatically corrected if you type or spell it incorrectly.

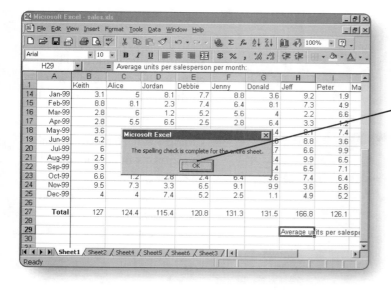

After Spelling is finished, a dialog box will appear telling you that the spell-check is complete for the entire sheet.

3. Click on **OK**. The dialog box will close.

6

Using Formulas and Functions

Merely entering large quantities of data into a worksheet isn't going to help you a great deal. You need to perform calculations on that data to summarize it in a useful way. For example, you might find it helpful to know how much you really spent this year on your car or phone bill. You can then apply the information to plan, budget, find trends, or make predictions. In this chapter, you'll learn how to:

- Use the Formula palette and functions to perform calculations
- Copy formulas with relative and absolute cell references
- Use Goal Seek to find information you need
- Use AutoCalculate and cell comments
- Correct errors in formulas

Entering a Simple Calculation

To add, subtract, multiply, or divide numbers, you can use formulas. Formulas use cell references combined with the addition (+), subtraction (-), multiplication (*), and division (/) operators to perform calculations.

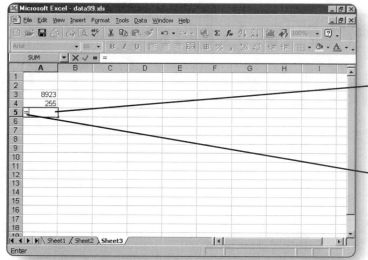

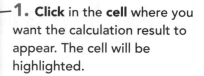

1. Click in the **cell** where you want the calculation result to appear. The cell will be highlighted.

2. Type an **equal sign** (=). Every formula must start with one.

3. Click on the **cell** with the first number you want to use. Excel will enter the cell address in the selected cell and Formula bar.

4. Type an **operator**. The operator you type will appear in the selected cell and in the Formula bar.

5. Click on the **cell** with the next value you want to use in your calculation. Excel will enter the cell address in the selected cell and Formula bar.

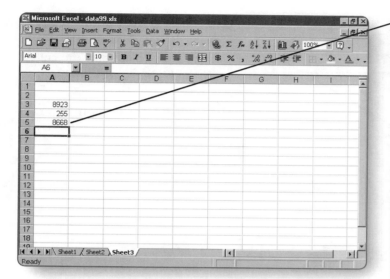

6. Press the **Enter key**. The result will be displayed in the selected cell.

NOTE
If a formula includes more than one operator, Excel calculates multiplication and division first, followed by addition and subtraction. However, you can use parentheses to control the order of precedence. Therefore, if you enter 1+2*3, the answer is 7, whereas if you enter (1+2)*3 the answer is 9.

Using Built-In Functions

Many calculations have been predefined in Excel. These built-in calculations are called *functions*. The easiest way to include a function in your worksheet is by using the Formula palette.

Using the Formula Palette with the SUM Function

The Formula palette keeps track of the functions you enter and displays a description of the formula and how it's constructed.

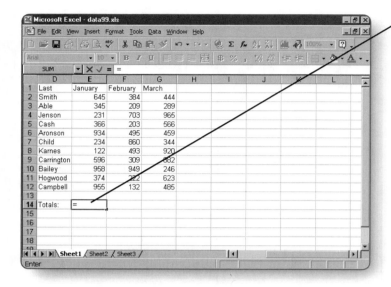

1. **Click** in the **cell** where you want the result of your calculation to appear. The cell will be highlighted.

2. **Type** an **equal sign**.

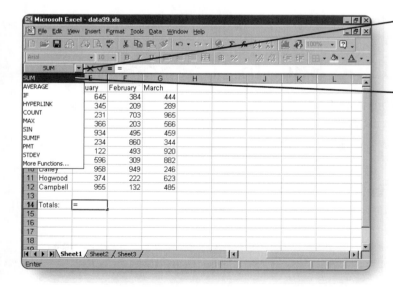

3. **Click** on the **down arrow** (▼) next to the Functions list. The list will drop down.

4. **Click** on **SUM**. The Formula palette will appear.

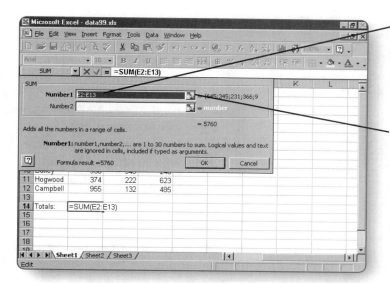

Notice that in the Number1 text box, Excel has tried to guess which numbers you're trying to add. If it is correct, you can skip steps 5 through 7.

5. Click on the **Collapse Dialog button** at the end of the Number1 text box to edit the formula. The Formula palette will shrink to allow you to see your worksheet and select the range of cells for the calculation.

6. Select the **cells** to be included in your calculation. A marquee will highlight your selection, and a range will appear in the Formula bar.

	Last	January	February	March
1	Last	January	February	March
2	Smith	645	384	444
3	Able	345	209	289
4	Jenson	231	703	965
5	Cash	366	203	566
6	Aronson	934	495	459
7	Child	234	860	344
8	Karnes	122	493	920
9	Carrington	596	309	882
10	Bailey	958	949	246
11	Hogwood	374	222	623
12	Campbell	955	132	485
13				
14	Totals:	=SUM(E2:E12)		

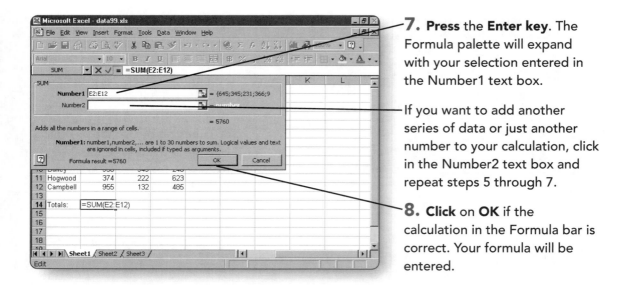

7. Press the **Enter key**. The Formula palette will expand with your selection entered in the Number1 text box.

If you want to add another series of data or just another number to your calculation, click in the Number2 text box and repeat steps 5 through 7.

8. Click on **OK** if the calculation in the Formula bar is correct. Your formula will be entered.

You can view the formula in the Formula bar and the total of the calculation in the selected cell.

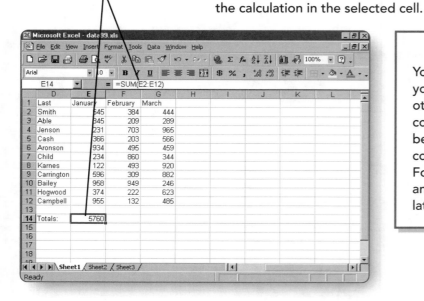

NOTE

You can copy the formula you just created to the other columns, and the copies will sum the numbers in their respective columns. See "Copying Formulas with Relative and Absolute References" later in this chapter.

Using AutoSum

AutoSum is a shortcut method of summing a column or row of numbers. It is faster than the method you just learned, but it works only with the SUM function.

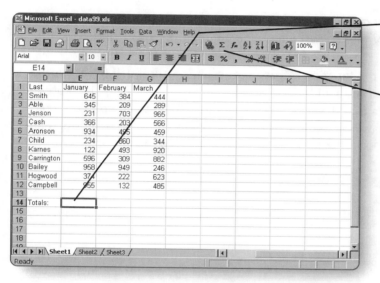

1. **Click** in the **cell** where you want a result. The cell will be highlighted.

2. **Click** on the **AutoSum button**. In the Formula bar, Excel will suggest a range to be added.

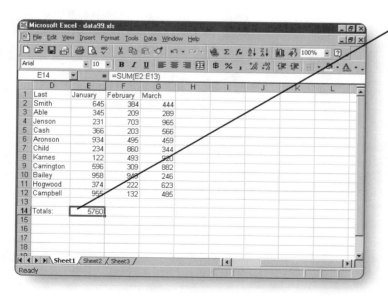

3. **Press** the **Enter key** if the range Excel suggests is correct. The result of the AutoSum will be entered in the selected cell.

If the suggested range is not correct, drag through the range you want before pressing the Enter key.

Creating an IF Function

All functions work in basically the same way. You enter the equal sign, select the function, and then tell the function which data to use. The next example demonstrates using a logical function rather than a mathematical one. Logical functions use the =, >, <, >=, <=, and <> operators within a formula to test whether something is true or false.

If the function is true, one result is returned; if false, another is returned. In the following example, a "Warning" is returned if it's true that you spent more than $200 to pay off your credit card account in a month. If it's false and you spent less than $200, "OK" is returned in the appropriate cell.

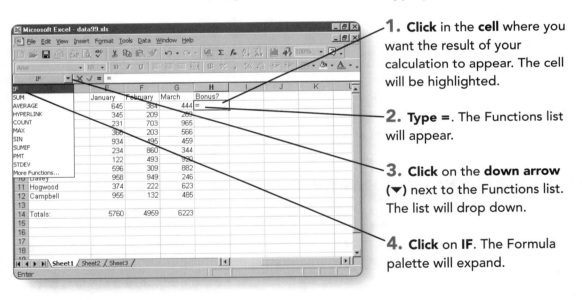

1. **Click** in the **cell** where you want the result of your calculation to appear. The cell will be highlighted.

2. **Type =**. The Functions list will appear.

3. **Click** on the **down arrow** (▼) next to the Functions list. The list will drop down.

4. **Click** on **IF**. The Formula palette will expand.

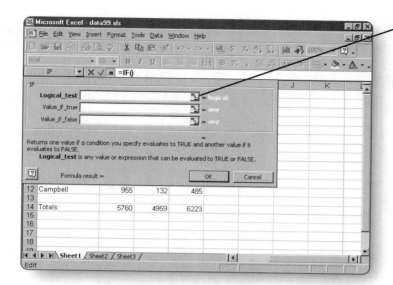

5. **Click** on the **Collapse Dialog button** at the end of the Logical_test text box. The Formula palette will shrink.

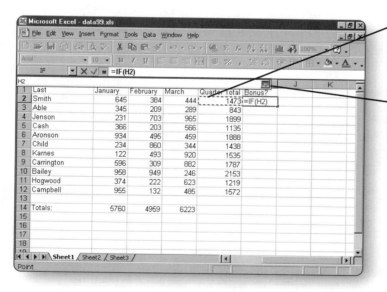

6. **Select** the **cell** or cells to evaluate. A flashing marquee will appear around the cell(s).

7. **Click** on the **Expand Dialog button** to expand the Formula palette. The selected range will be entered in the text box.

8. Type the **condition** in the Logical_test text box. For example, to test whether the value is greater than 1200, **type >1200**.

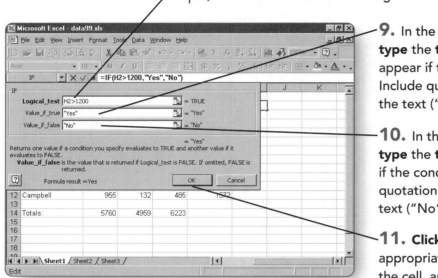

9. In the Value_if_true box, **type** the **text** you want to appear if the condition is true. Include quotation marks around the text ("Yes").

10. In the Value_if_false box, **type** the **text** you want returned if the condition is false. Include quotation marks around the text ("No").

11. Click on **OK**. The appropriate text will appear in the cell, and the formula you entered will appear in the Formula bar.

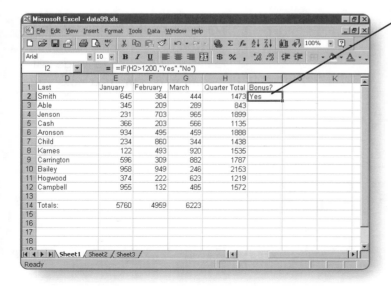

12. Drag the **Fill handle** across a row or column to copy the formula. Results of the same formula for each of the other rows will appear.

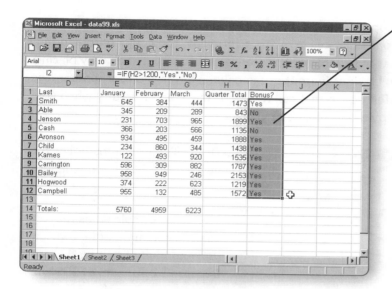

In rows where the value in column H is less than or equal to 1200, column I reports "No"; it shows "Yes" when the value is greater than 1200.

Copying Formulas with Relative and Absolute References

When you copy a formula, the copy changes depending on where you put it. It is therefore said to be *relative*. You saw this at work in the last two steps of the preceding procedure. When you copied the formula from cell I2 into cells I3 through I12, the reference to cell H2 changed to refer to cells H3 through H12, respectively.

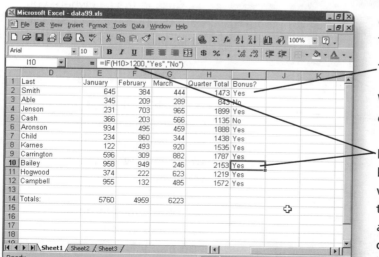

The formula in I2 refers to H2.

When that formula is copied to cell I10, it refers to cell H10.

Most of the time you will want Excel to copy formulas in this way. However, there may be times when you want an *absolute* cell reference, which does not change depending on location.

Suppose, for example, that you want to include a reference to a particular cell in multiple formulas. You could write a formula that marks that cell reference as an absolute value by placing dollar signs in front of the column letter and row number. The reference to that cell will then stay fixed (absolute) when you copy the formula elsewhere.

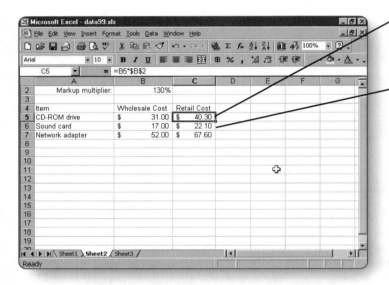

This cell's formula multiplies the number in B5 by the multiplier in B2.

This cell's formula takes the value in column B of its own row (B6) and multiplies it by B2. Because B2 appears as B2 in the formula, the reference does not change when the formula is copied to different locations.

To set up a formula like the one in the preceding example, use the following procedure.

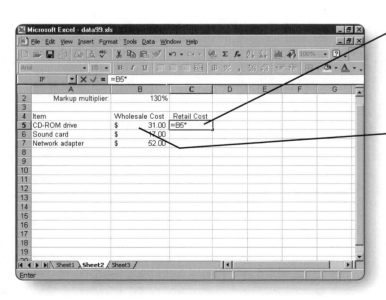

1. Click in the **cell** where you want the formula. The cell will be highlighted.

2. Type =.

3. Click on the **cell** that you want to use for the first part of the formula. This is the cell that *will* change when you copy the formula.

4. Type a **math operator symbol** to indicate the math operator you want.

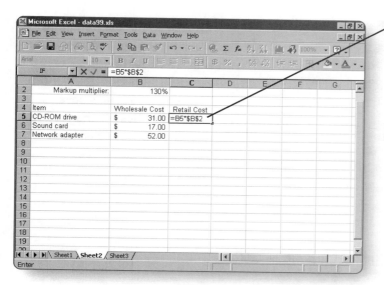

5. Type a **dollar sign ($)**.

6. Type the **column letter** for the cell that should have an absolute reference.

7. Type another **$**.

8. Type the **row number** for the cell that should have an absolute reference.

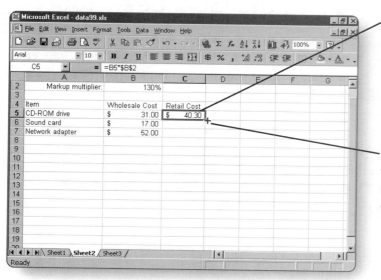

9. Press the **Enter key**. The formula result will appear in the cell.

10. Click on the **cell** containing the formula again to re-select it.

11. Point at the **Fill handle** in the bottom-right corner of the selected cell. The mouse pointer will become a cross.

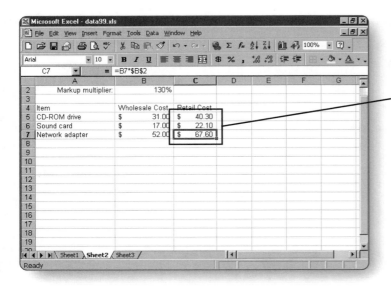

12. **Drag** the **Fill handle** to highlight the cells where you want to copy the formula.

The copied formulas have different values for the first cell reference, but they all have B2 as the second cell reference.

NOTE

When you are creating or editing a formula, position your insertion point within a cell reference and then press F4 to cycle through the available combinations of relative and absolute references. For example, if the reference is to cell B2, pressing the F4 key produces B2, B$2, and $B2, sequentially. Stop pressing F4 when the value you want appears.

Using the Goal Seek Tool

The Goal Seek tool enables you to find a result by adjusting one of the cells in a worksheet. First, you need to specify a goal and then tell Excel what cell's value it can adjust to meet that goal.

Suppose that you are tracking your budget in Excel, and you want to know how much money is left after paying your expenses to be deposited into your Savings account. Your goal is to "balance," or have your monthly income minus monthly expenses equal zero (0).

1. **Click** in the **cell** that you want to change to the new goal value. The cell will be highlighted.

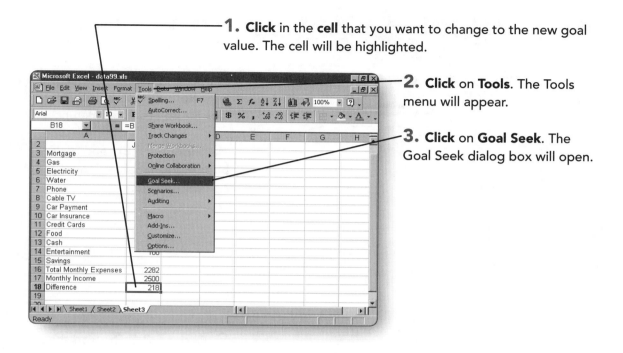

2. **Click** on **Tools**. The Tools menu will appear.

3. **Click** on **Goal Seek**. The Goal Seek dialog box will open.

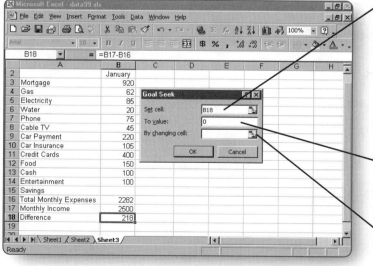

The address of the cell that will contain the goal value should already appear in the Set cell: text box. If not, type in the correct cell reference.

4. **Click** in the **To value**: text box.

5. **Type** the new **goal value** for the cell mentioned in the To Value: text box.

6. **Click** on the **Collapse Dialog button** next to By changing cell:.

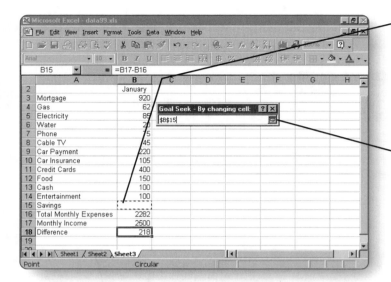

7. Click in the **cell** that you want to adjust.

In this case, it's the Savings cell, B15. Notice the $ signs that indicate an absolute reference.

8. Click on the **Expand Dialog button**. The Goal Seek dialog box will expand.

9. Click on **OK**. The worksheet will recalculate.

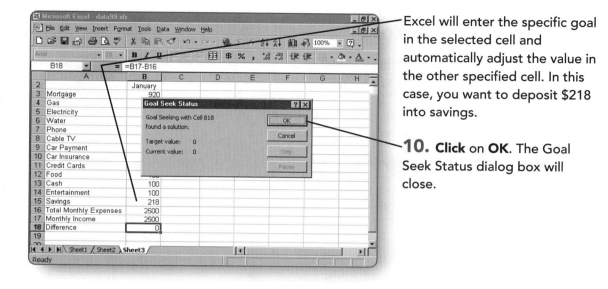

Excel will enter the specific goal in the selected cell and automatically adjust the value in the other specified cell. In this case, you want to deposit $218 into savings.

10. **Click** on **OK**. The Goal Seek Status dialog box will close.

Using AutoCalculate

You might find that occasionally you want to know the sum or average of a group of numbers but don't really need to record the information in a worksheet. By default, the sum of a group of selected cells appears automatically in the status bar, but you can change that to Average, Count, or one of several other common calculations.

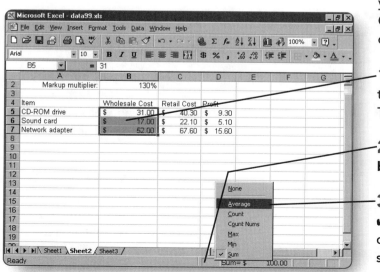

1. **Select** the **cells** containing the values you want to calculate. The cells will be highlighted.

2. **Right-click** on the **status bar**. A pop-up menu will appear.

3. **Click** on a **function** to put a ✔ by it. The result of the calculation will appear in the status bar.

Adding Comments

When you begin to build larger, more complex calculations, it is sometimes useful to include an explanation of what you've done, but you may not want those explanations cluttering up your worksheet. One way to add information is to include a comment.

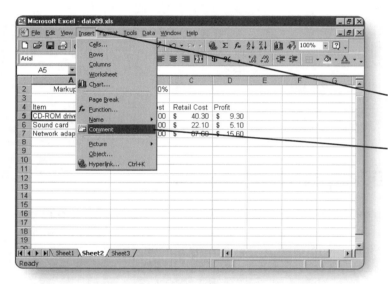

1. Click on the **cell** where you want to include the comment. The cell will be highlighted.

2. Click on **Insert**. The Insert menu will appear.

3. Click on **Comment**. A text box will open with a flashing insertion point.

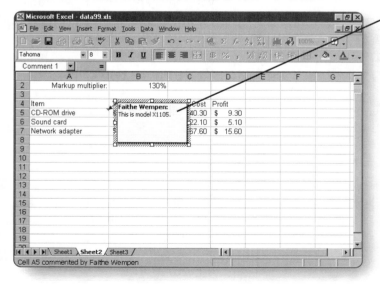

4. Type your **comment**.

5. Click anywhere outside the comment box. The comment box will disappear, but a tiny red triangle will appear in the top-right corner of the cell.

NOTE

To view the comment, move the mouse pointer over the triangle, and the comment box will pop up.

Some Common Mistakes to Avoid

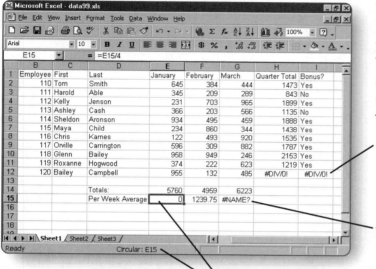

The Formula palette helps beginners avoid mistakes, but you'll probably still make a few. When you make a mistake, a number of error messages might appear. The following are the most common:

- **#DIV/0!**. This means that you've tried to divide by either an empty cell or one containing 0.

- **#NAME?**. This may mean that you deleted information referred to in your formula.

- **Circular**. This means that a formula in a cell refers to the same cell. You may see a blue dot in a cell containing a circular reference.

When you check your formulas, some things to watch for are that:

- Formulas start with an equal sign.
- All the necessary parentheses are included.
- You referred to the correct cells.
- You've included all the arguments for a function and no extra arguments.

NOTE

You may find the Auditing toolbar handy in resolving worksheet errors. To display it, open the Tools menu, point to Auditing, and click on Show Auditing Toolbar. For more information about the tools on this toolbar, see the Excel 2000 Help system, or use What's This? Help as described in Chapter 2, "What's on the Excel Screen?"

7

Navigating Your Worksheets

As you create larger worksheets, it's possible to get lost in the flood of data and not know exactly where you are. Fortunately, Excel has features to help you work with larger worksheets. In this chapter, you'll learn how to:

- Name a range
- Move directly to a specific cell or range
- Find and replace entries in your worksheet
- Hide and display rows and columns
- Split your Excel window and freeze parts of a worksheet

Naming a Range

Naming a range is useful because names are easier to read and remember than cell addresses. Named ranges can be used to quickly select text and move around a worksheet in combination with the Go To command. They can also be used in formulas.

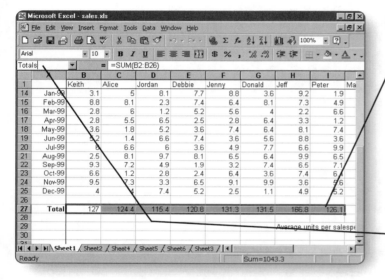

1. **Click** in a **cell** or **drag** the **mouse arrow** across a **range** of **cells**. The cell(s) will be highlighted.

2. **Click** in the **Name text box** to the left of the Formula bar. The text box will be highlighted.

3. **Type** a **name** for the highlighted cells.

4. **Press** the **Enter key**. The name will appear in the Name text box.

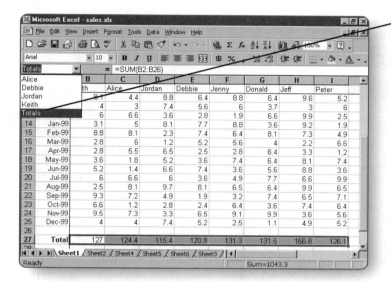

To quickly select a named cell or range, click on the down arrow (▼) at the end of the Name text box and select from the drop-down list.

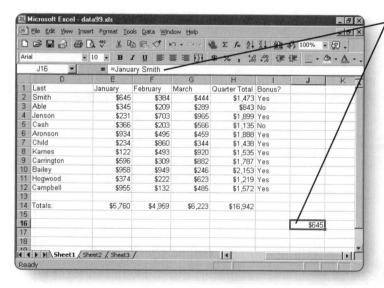

You can also name entire rows and columns, and then use those names to find the value contained in the cell at their intersection. For example, suppose that you named column E "January" and row 2 "Smith." You could then enter a formula anywhere in the worksheet **=January Smith** that would pull the value from cell E2. (The space between January and Smith is called the *intersection operator*.) Such formulas are absolute and do not change when you move or copy them.

Moving Directly to a Cell or Range

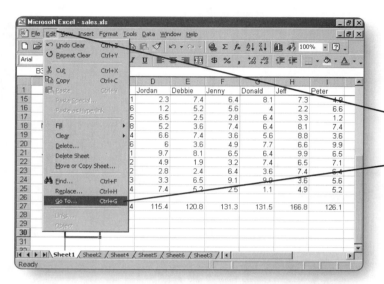

When you have thousands of entries in your worksheet, moving with the arrow keys or scroll bar can be frustrating.

1. Click on **Edit**. The Edit menu will appear.

2. Click on **Go To**. The Go To dialog box will open.

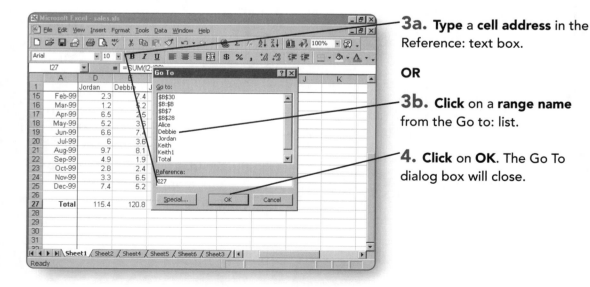

3a. Type a **cell address** in the Reference: text box.

OR

3b. Click on a **range name** from the Go to: list.

4. Click on **OK**. The Go To dialog box will close.

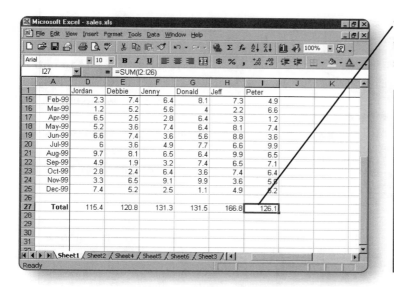

The cell or range you specified will become the active cell or selected range.

TIP

To move to the last cell that contains data in a worksheet, press the Ctrl and End keys at the same time. To move back to the first cell (A1), press the Ctrl and Home keys at the same time.

Finding and Replacing Cell Entries

If you need to update your worksheet (maybe interest rates have increased), you can use the Find or Replace commands to help you.

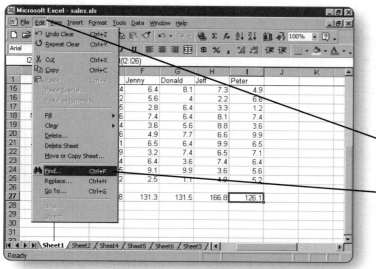

Finding Cell Entries

To modify data in your worksheet, you must first find the cell (or cells) that contains the data you want to change.

1. Click on **Edit**. The Edit menu will appear.

2. Click on **Find**. The Find dialog box will open.

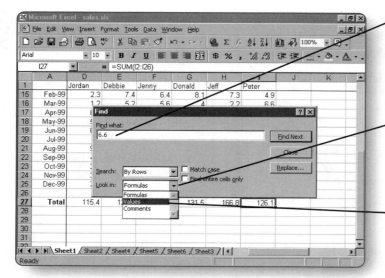

3. **Type** the **word** or **number** you want to find in the Find what: text box. Be sure to enter it exactly as it was originally entered into the worksheet.

4. **Click** on the **down arrow** (▼) next to the Look in: text box. The Look in: drop-down list will appear.

5. **Click** on **Formulas**, **Values**, or **Comments**, depending on what kind of data you want Find to search.

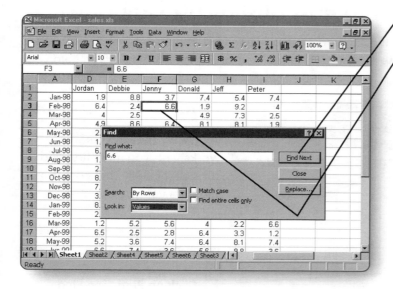

6. **Click** on **Find Next**.

Excel will find the first occurrence of the word or number. You can continue to click on Find Next until all occurrences have been identified.

Replacing Cell Entries

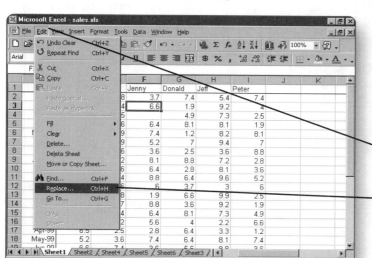

When a cell that needs to be modified is found, you can use Excel to automatically replace the data for you without your having to manually enter the changes.

1. Click on **Edit**. The Edit menu will appear.

2. Click on **Replace**. The Replace dialog box will open.

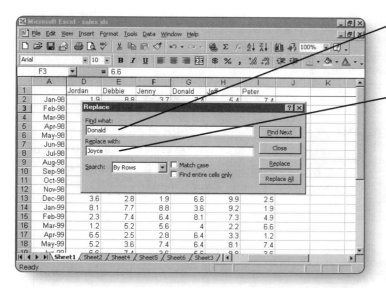

3. Type the **word** or **number** you want to replace in the Find what: text box.

4. Type the **revised entry** in the Replace with: text box.

NOTE

At this point, you can click on Replace All and immediately replace all occurrences of the original entry with the new one. However, it's not a good idea to do this if you're not an experienced user. You may replace something you didn't intend to replace.

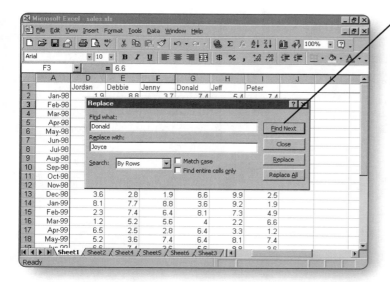

5. Click on **Find Next**. Excel will find the first occurrence of the word or number.

6a. Click on **Replace**. The item will be replaced.

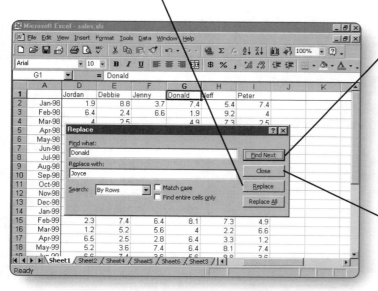

OR

6b. Click on **Find Next**. Excel will find the next occurrence of the word or number.

7. Repeat steps 5 and **6** until you've checked all occurrences of the word or number in the worksheet.

8. Click on **Close**. The dialog box will close.

Viewing Different Parts of Your Worksheet at the Same Time

When your worksheet is bigger than the area you can see on your screen at one time, it becomes difficult to remember where exactly you are as you move down or across a worksheet and can no longer see the row and column labels you entered. Are you in the January or February column, or the cash or sales row? You can manipulate a worksheet in several ways to overcome this problem.

Hiding Rows and Columns

If your worksheet has columns or rows that you really don't need to work in anymore, or that you don't want to print, you can hide them.

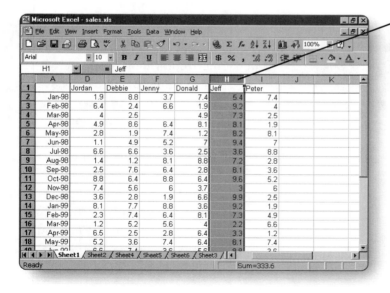

1. **Select** the **column** or **row** to hide. The column or row will be highlighted.

2. Click on **Format**. The Format menu will appear.

3. Click on **Column** or **Row**. A submenu will appear.

4. Click on **Hide**. The column or row will be hidden.

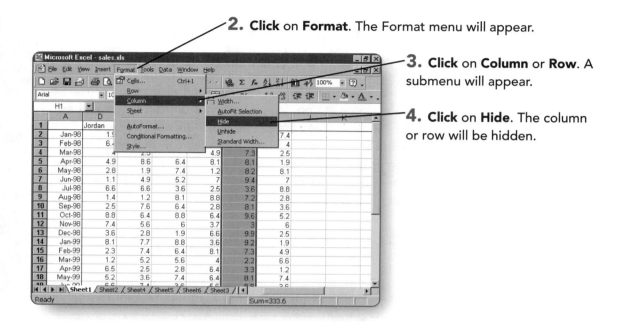

Initially, a dark vertical or horizontal line will appear where the columns or rows you have hidden were. This is the hidden column or row, still selected.

However, once you move in the worksheet, the dark line disappears and the only way to tell that rows or columns have been hidden is by the missing letters or numbers in the row or column headers.

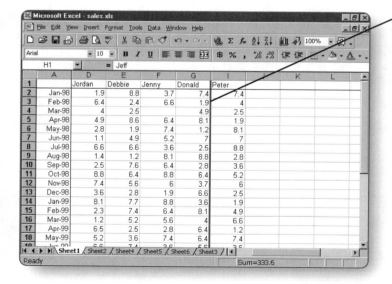

Displaying Hidden Rows or Columns

If you decide you do need to see those hidden rows or columns, you can make them reappear in the worksheet.

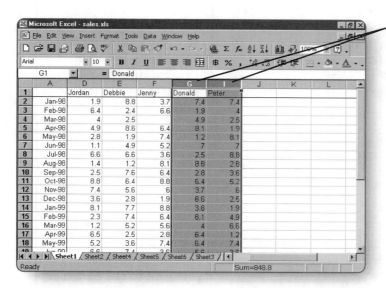

1. **Select** the **rows** or **columns** on both sides of the missing rows or columns. The cells will be highlighted.

2. **Click** on **Format**. The Format menu will appear.

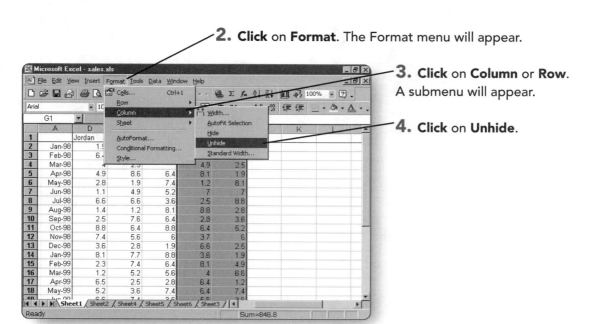

3. **Click** on **Column** or **Row**. A submenu will appear.

4. **Click** on **Unhide**.

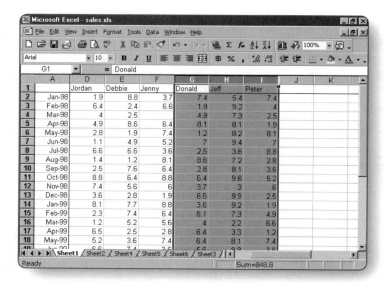

The missing columns or rows will reappear.

Splitting a Window

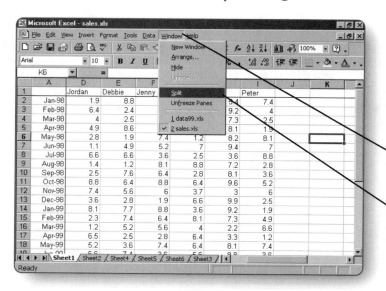

If you want to see particular sections of the same worksheet, but the worksheet is so big that you can't view both sections onscreen at the same time, you can split a window.

1. Click on **Window**. The Window menu will appear.

2. Click on **Split**. The spreadsheet will be divided into four sections.

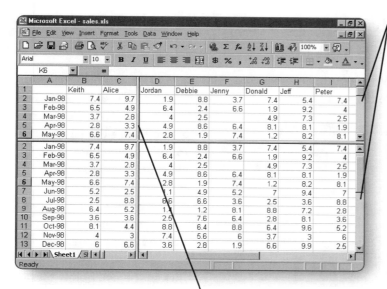

When you split, each pane has its own scroll bars. You can scroll each pane and/or drag the split bars to reposition them on the screen.

3. Adjust the **view** of your worksheet in each window with the four scroll bars until you can see what you want to compare.

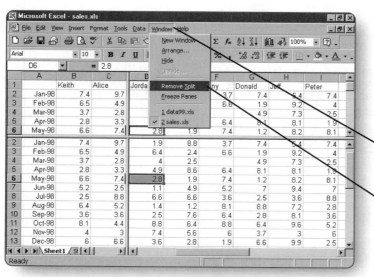

Removing a Split

If you no longer need the split view, you can remove the split so that your screen shows only one section of the worksheet.

1. Click on **Window**. The Window menu will appear.

2. Click on **Remove Split**. The split will be removed.

Keeping Row or Column Labels Visible

When you're entering data, you need to know which row and column you're on. The letters and numbers Excel provides are not very informative. You need to be able to see the labels you set up for certain columns and rows, such as months of the year or employee names. You can do this by freezing columns and rows that contain labels you need to see all the time.

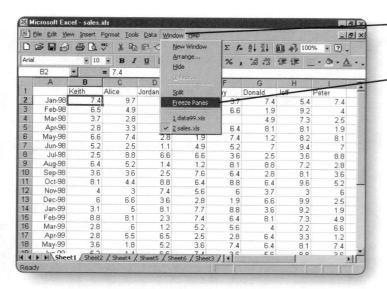

1. Click in the **cell** below the column labels and to the right of the row labels. The cell will be highlighted.

2. Click on **Window**. The Window menu will appear.

3. Click on **Freeze Panes**. The column and row labels will stay onscreen while you work with the spreadsheet.

Notice when you scroll left and right through your data, the column containing the row labels remains onscreen. When you scroll up and down through your data, the row containing the column labels remains frozen onscreen. However, if you scroll left and right, the column labels move, and if you scroll up and down, the row labels move.

Removing the Freeze

If you do not need to see column and row labels all the time, you can remove the freeze so that the column and row labels scroll as usual.

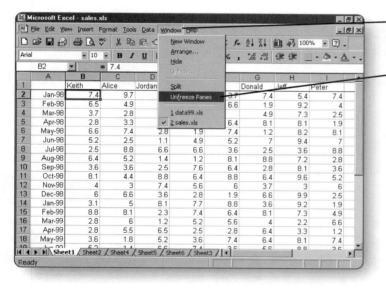

1. Click on **Window**. The Window menu will appear.

2. Click on **Unfreeze Panes**. The column and row labels will now move as you work with the spreadsheet.

8

Using Macros

Whenever you find yourself repeating the same keystrokes again and again, you can probably benefit from a macro. A *macro* is simply a recording of keystrokes, and in the same way that you play recordings of music, you can play macros. In this chapter, you'll learn how to:

- Create and name a macro
- Run a macro
- Delete a macro

Recording and Naming Your Macro

Before recording a macro, plan what you intend to include. If you make mistakes while recording, all the mistakes will be recorded along with the correct keystrokes.

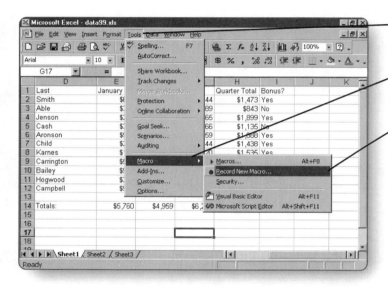

1. Click on **Tools**. The Tools menu will appear.

2. Click on **Macro**. A submenu will appear.

3. Click on **Record New Macro**. The Record Macro dialog box will open.

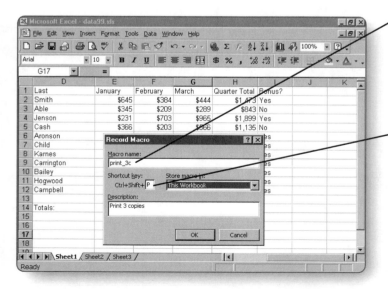

4. Type a **name** for your macro in the Macro name: text box. No spaces are allowed; use an underscore (_) to simulate spaces as needed.

5. Type a **letter** in the Shortcut key: text box for the shortcut key for your macro. You can press the Shift key as you type the letter to include Shift in the key combination.

6. Type a **description** for your macro in the Description: text box. The description will appear in the Macro dialog box when you run the macro.

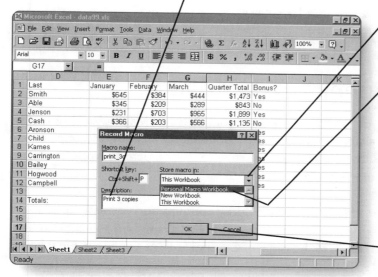

7. Click on the **down arrow (▼)** to the right of Store macro in:. A drop-down menu will appear.

8. Click on **Personal Macro Workbook**, **New Workbook**, or **This Workbook** to store your macro. Personal Macro Workbook is the best solution because you will probably want to have this macro available for use with all your worksheets.

9. Click on **OK**. The macro will be saved.

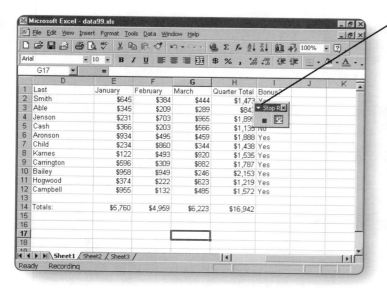

The Stop Recording toolbar appears. From now until you click on the Stop Recording button, everything you do in Excel is recorded as part of the macro.

10. Perform steps you want to record for your macro.

11. Click on the **Stop Recording button**. The macro will be saved.

NOTE

If you make mistakes while performing steps, it is best just to delete your macro and start again. See the section "Deleting Macros" for help.

Running Your Macro

If you saved the macro in your Personal Macro Workbook, it is available in every worksheet you create. If not, you must make the correct worksheet active for your macro to work. To run your macro, you can:

1a. Press the **shortcut key combination** you assigned for the macro. The macro will run. For example, if the shortcut is Ctrl+Shift+P, hold down Ctrl and Shift as you press the P key.

OR

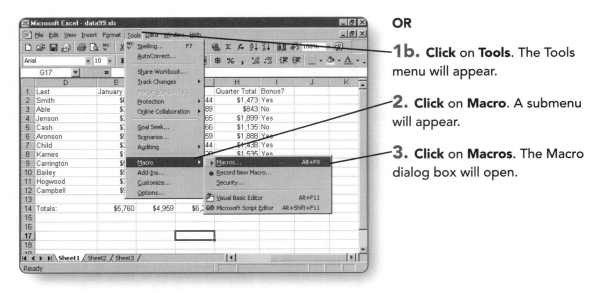

1b. Click on **Tools**. The Tools menu will appear.

2. Click on **Macro**. A submenu will appear.

3. Click on **Macros**. The Macro dialog box will open.

4. Click on the **name** of the macro you want to run. The name will be highlighted.

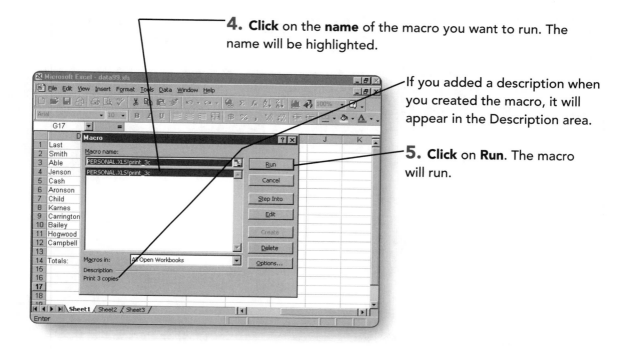

If you added a description when you created the macro, it will appear in the Description area.

5. Click on **Run**. The macro will run.

Deleting Macros

As stated previously, macros are either stored with a worksheet or in your Personal Macro Workbook. You need to have the appropriate worksheet or workbook open to delete a macro. If you saved your macro with a specific worksheet, simply open the worksheet.

Displaying the Personal Macro Workbook

If you saved your macro in the Personal Macro Workbook, which is automatically opened when you start Excel, you need to unhide the workbook.

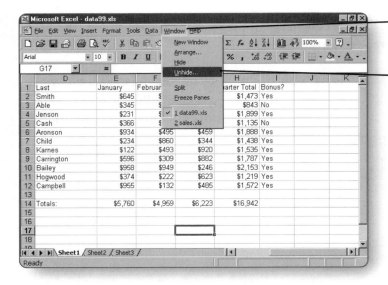

1. Click on **Window**. The Window menu will appear.

2. Click on **Unhide**. The Unhide dialog box will open.

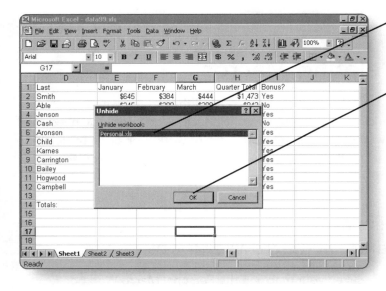

3. Click on **Personal** in the Unhide workbook: text box. The item will be highlighted.

4. Click on **OK**. The workbook will open.

Deleting a Macro with a Workbook or Worksheet Open

When you have the workbook or worksheet open, you can then delete the macro.

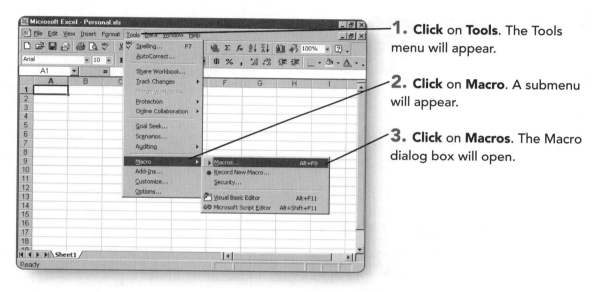

1. **Click** on **Tools**. The Tools menu will appear.

2. **Click** on **Macro**. A submenu will appear.

3. **Click** on **Macros**. The Macro dialog box will open.

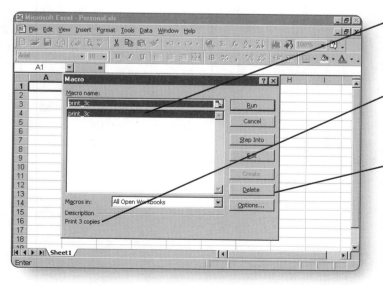

4. **Click** on the **macro** you want to delete. The name will be highlighted.

Check the description so that you are sure you are deleting the correct macro.

5. **Click** on **Delete**. A dialog box will open that asks whether you want to delete the macro.

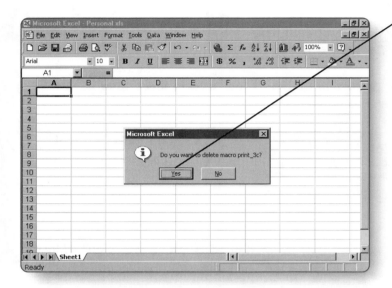

6. **Click** on **Yes**. The macro will be deleted.

Hiding the Personal Macro Workbook

After deleting a macro, you can then hide the Personal Macro Workbook.

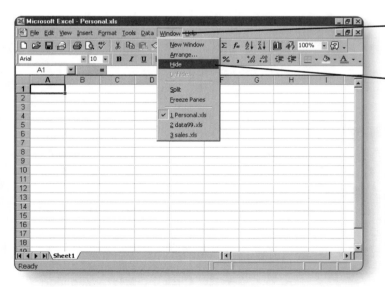

1. **Click** on **Window**. The Window menu will appear.

2. **Click** on **Hide**. The workbook will be hidden.

NOTE

If you don't hide the Personal Macro Workbook while you're working in Excel, the next time you open the program it will be hidden.

9

Working with Data

Excel can be used not only to perform calculations but also to store data that you can then sort and search to find information and make decisions. In this chapter, you'll learn how to:

- Sort data by rows and columns
- Search for information that meets specific criteria
- Protect you data

Sorting Data

If you enter a large amount of data into a worksheet, it may be easier to find information you need by sorting your data. You can easily sort data in Excel either alphabetically or numerically, in ascending or descending order.

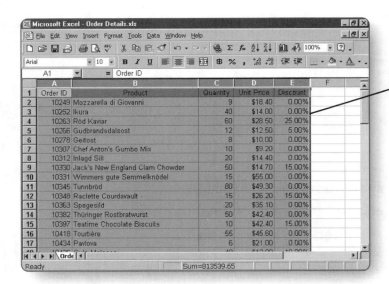

Sorting the Order of Rows in a Range

1. **Click** and **drag** the **mouse arrow** to highlight the cells of the range you want to sort. In this example, all the columns that contain data have been selected.

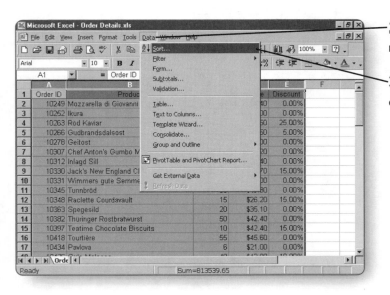

2. **Click** on **Data**. The Data menu will appear.

3. **Click** on **Sort**. The Sort dialog box will open.

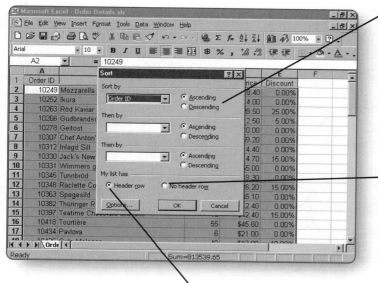

4. Click on **Ascending** or **Descending** in the Sort by box. Ascending will sort alphabetically, A through Z or numerically, smallest to largest. Descending will do the opposite: Z through A and largest to smallest.

5a. Click on **No header row** if your selection does not include the row that contains the column headings.

OR

5b. Click on **Header row** if you do have a header row.

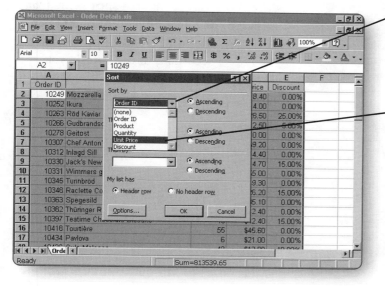

6. Click on the **down arrow** (▼) next to the Sort by drop-down list. The list of options to sort by will appear.

7. Click on the **name** of the **column** by which you want to sort. If you chose Header row in step 5, the names of the headers will appear on this drop-down list; if you chose No header row, the column letters will appear.

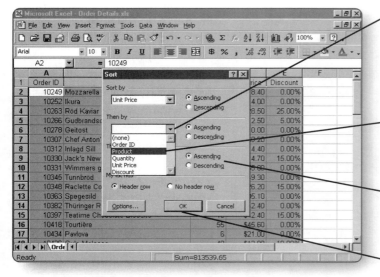

8. Click on the **down arrow [▼]** next to the Then by list if you want to sort by another column in the event of a "tie" in the primary sort column.

9. Click on the **name** of the **column** to use for the secondary sort.

10. Click on **Ascending** or **Descending** for the secondary sort.

11. Click on **OK**. The dialog box will close.

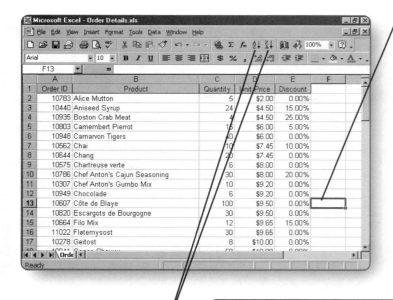

12. Click on a **spot away from the selection area** to deselect the cells. The data will be sorted according to the criteria you specified.

TIP

You can also sort using the Sort Ascending and Sort Descending toolbar buttons to sort by the single column that contains the cell cursor.

Sorting the Order of Columns in a Range

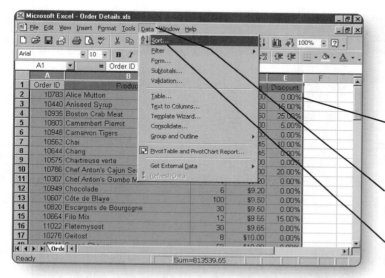

The following steps change the order of the columns from left to right, without affecting the order in which the records (the rows) appear.

1. Click and **drag** the **mouse arrow** to highlight the cells of the range you want to sort.

2. Click on **Data**. The Data menu will appear.

3. Click on **Sort**. The Sort dialog box will open.

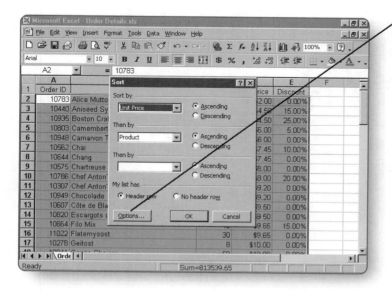

4. Click on **Options**. The Sort Options dialog box will open.

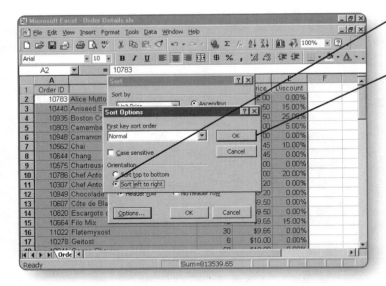

5. Click on **Sort left to right** in the Orientation section.

6. Click on **OK**. The Sort Options dialog box will close, and you will be returned to the Sort dialog box.

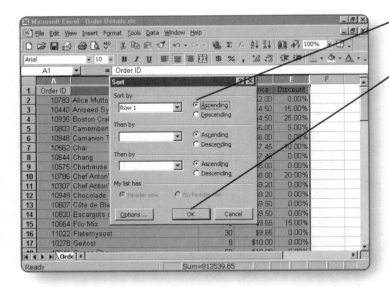

7. Click on **Ascending** in the Sort by box.

8. Click on **OK**. The Sort dialog box will close.

The data will appear sorted alphabetically by column head, left to right.

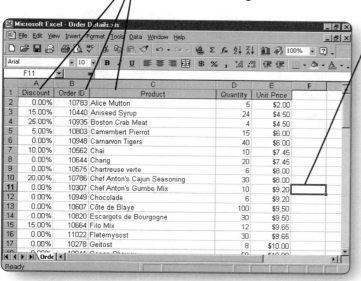

9. **Click** anywhere **away** from the selected range. The cells will be deselected.

Filtering Data

You can search for data using the Filter command to select information that meets criteria of your choosing. For example, you can set up a filter that will search through prices and pull up all products that are less than $30.

1. **Click** on the **column head** that you want to use in your search. The cell will be highlighted.

2. **Click** on **Data**. The Data menu will appear.

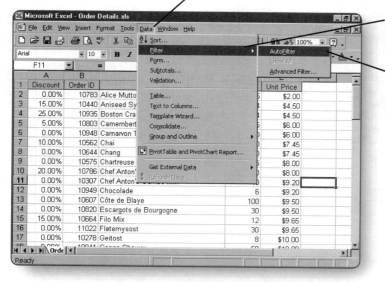

3. **Click** on **Filter**. A submenu will appear.

4. **Click** on **AutoFilter**. AutoFilter arrows will appear next to the column heads.

You can filter by any field, but for this example, the criterion you will set is Unit Price under $30.

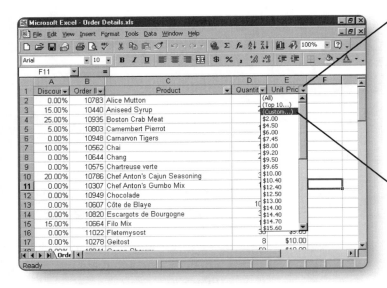

5. Click on the **down arrow** (▼) in the column for Unit Price. All the entries in the Unit Price column will appear in the drop-down list. You can select any of the options in the list to see only those rows in the worksheet.

6. Click on **Custom**. A criterion for selecting rows in the worksheet will be set up. The custom AutoFilter dialog box will open.

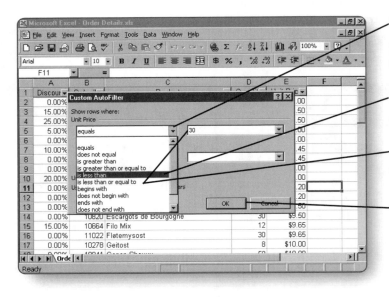

7. Click on the **down arrow** (▼) next to "equals." A drop-down list will appear.

8. Click on **is less than**. Your selection will be highlighted.

9. Tab to the **next text box** to the right and **type $30**.

10. Click on **OK**.

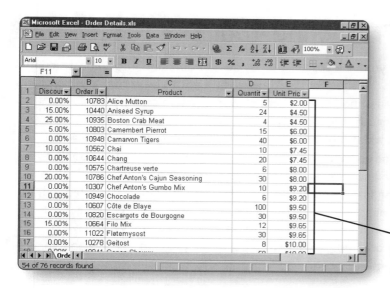

TIP

You can continue to refine your requirements in the custom AutoFilter dialog box. For example, you could search for less than $400 and more than $350 using "And" with the additional text boxes.

The worksheet will now only show products that meet the criterion of being less than $30.

Turning Off AutoFilter

When you are finished using AutoFilter, it's easy to turn it off.

1. Click on **Data**. The Data menu will appear.

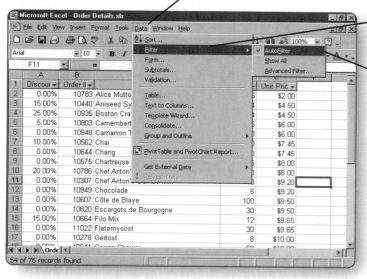

2. Click on **Filter**. A submenu will appear.

3. Click on **AutoFilter**. The worksheet will appear as it was before the search.

Protecting Your Data

If you've invested a great deal of time and effort constructing a worksheet or workbook, you want to be sure that no one can either by accident, or worse, intentionally, make unauthorized changes to your data. You can protect your work at the worksheet level by allowing others to view but not edit the sheet without a password. At the workbook level, you can prevent worksheets from being moved, hidden, or renamed; and windows from being moved, resized, hidden, or closed. Be aware that if you lose the password, you cannot gain access to the files, data, or options you've password protected. Always write down the password and keep it in a secure place.

Protecting Your Worksheet

You can protect the integrity of the data in your worksheet by setting up password protection.

1. **Click** on **Tools**. The Tools menu will appear.

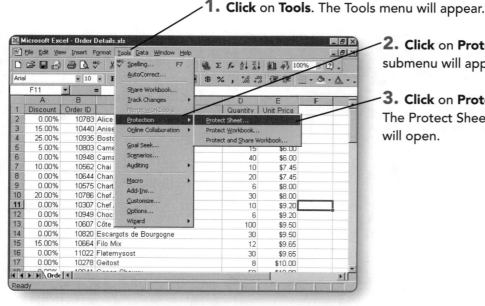

2. **Click** on **Protection**. A submenu will appear.

3. **Click** on **Protect Sheet**. The Protect Sheet dialog box will open.

4. Click on a **check box** (Contents, Objects, or Scenarios). A ✔ will appear next to the check box(es) chosen.

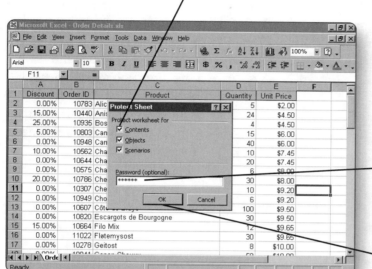

5. Type a **password** in the Password box. A series of asterisks will appear in the box rather than the actual password.

6. Click on **OK**. The Confirm Password dialog box will open.

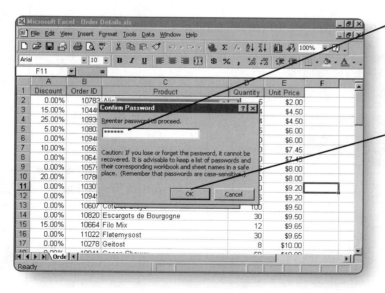

7. Type the **password** again to ensure you typed it correctly the first time. A series of asterisks will appear in the Reenter password to proceed box.

8. Click on **OK**. The Confirm Password dialog box will close.

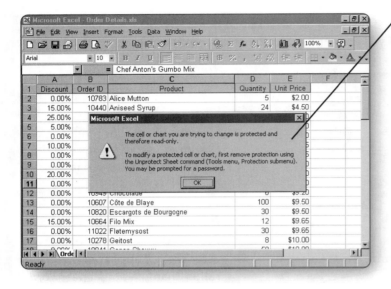

The worksheet can be opened and viewed, but if someone tries to change the data, a prompt will be displayed that says the worksheet is password protected. To remove the protection, you must choose Tools, Protection, Unprotect Sheet and enter the password. Without the password, changes cannot be made.

Removing Password Protection from Worksheets

As important as password protection is, sometimes you need to remove it from your worksheets.

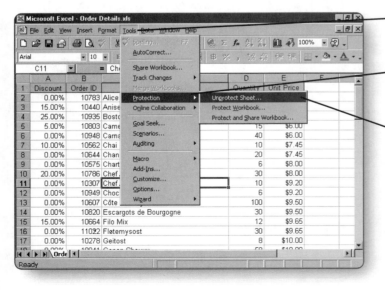

1. Click on **Tools**. The Tools menu will appear.

2. Click on **Protection**. A submenu will appear.

3. Click on **Unprotect Sheet**. The Unprotect Sheet dialog box will open.

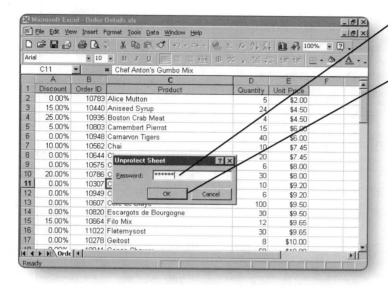

4. **Type** the **password** in the Password: text box.

5. **Click** on **OK**. The worksheet will be unprotected.

Protecting Your Workbook

You can also protect your worksheets at the workbook or file level.

1. **Click** on **Tools**. The Tools menu will appear.

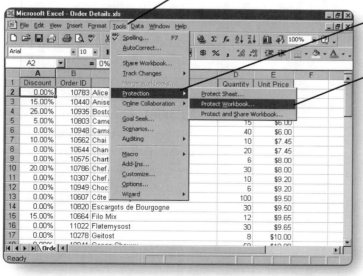

2. **Click** on **Protection**. A submenu will appear.

3. **Click** on **Protect Workbook**. The Protect Workbook dialog box will open.

4. **Click** on **Structure** to put a ✔ next to it if there is not already one there. This will prevent the worksheets from being moved, hidden, or renamed, and new sheets from being added.

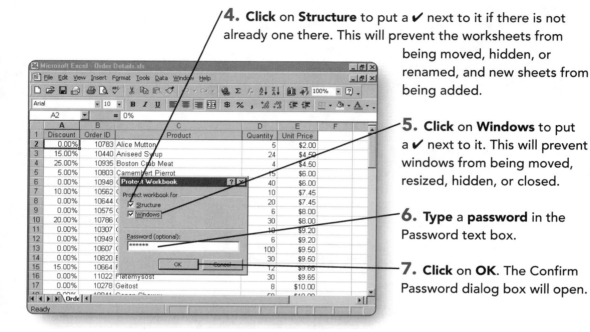

5. **Click** on **Windows** to put a ✔ next to it. This will prevent windows from being moved, resized, hidden, or closed.

6. **Type** a **password** in the Password text box.

7. **Click** on **OK**. The Confirm Password dialog box will open.

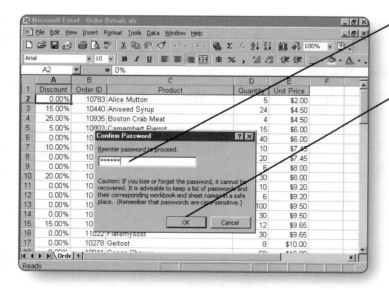

8. **Type** the **password** again to ensure that you typed it correctly the first time.

9. **Click** on **OK**. The Confirm Password dialog box will close. Now all commands related to modifying the structure of the workbook or the windows in the workbook will be unavailable (dimmed on the menus) as long as the protection is on.

Removing Password Protection from Workbooks

You must also know how to remove password protection for your workbooks.

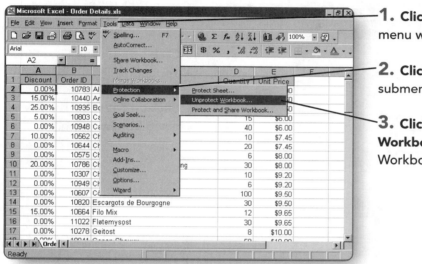

1. Click on **Tools**. The Tools menu will appear.

2. Click on **Protection**. A submenu will appear.

3. Click on **Unprotect Workbook**. The Unprotect Workbook dialog box will open.

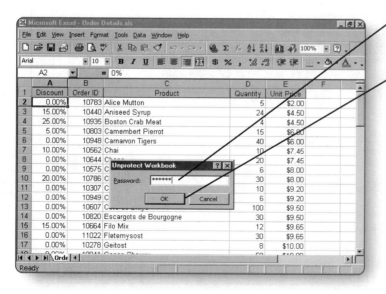

4. Type the **password** in the Password: text box.

5. Click on **OK**. The workbook will be unprotected.

Preventing Your Workbook from Being Opened

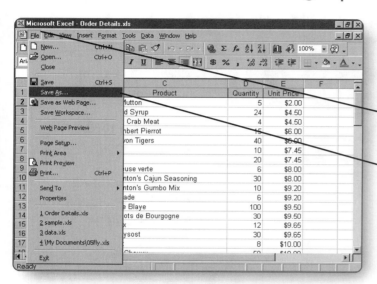

You can also set a password to prevent other people from opening your workbooks altogether.

1. Click on **File**. The File menu will appear.

2. Click on **Save As**. The Save As dialog box will open.

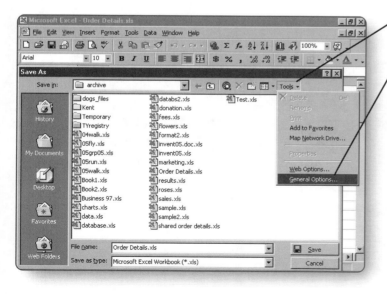

3. Click on **Tools**. A menu will open.

4. Click on **General Options**. The Save Options dialog box will open.

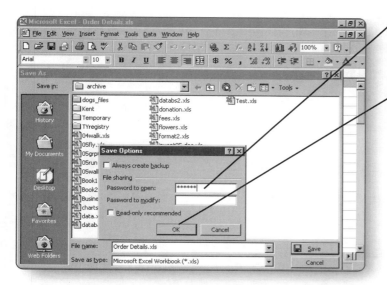

5. Type a **password** in the Password to open: text box. Passwords are case-sensitive.

6. Click on **OK**. The Confirm Password dialog box will open.

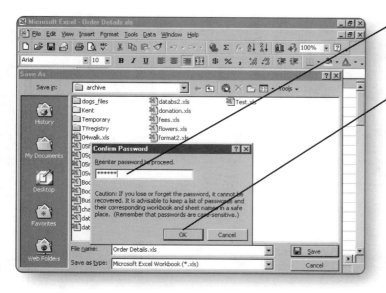

7. Type the **password** again in the Reenter password to proceed text box.

8. Click on **OK**. The Save As dialog box will appear.

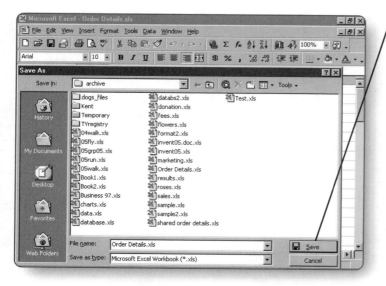

9. **Click** on **Save**. A prompt will appear.

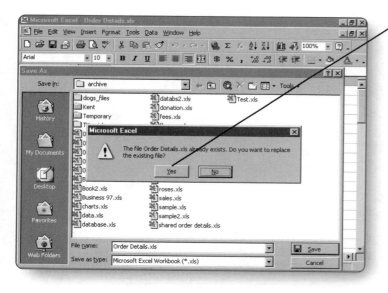

10. **Click** on **Yes**. The existing workbook will be replaced.

10

Working with Wizards and Templates

Wizards and templates make working with Excel much easier. *Wizards* ask you for relevant information and then perform a task for you, whereas *templates* are built-in forms that enable you to produce professional-looking documents such as invoices with just a few keystrokes. In this chapter, you'll learn how to:

- Use a wizard
- Open a template
- Customize a template
- Create a document using a template

Using a Wizard

Wizards help you perform difficult tasks by prompting you for required information and then performing a task for you. Several Excel wizards are available to you. The Lookup Wizard helps you write a formula that finds the value at the intersection of a row and column. The File Conversion Wizard helps you convert files created in other programs, such as Lotus 1-2-3, so that you can use them in Excel. The Web Form Wizard configures your worksheet so that it can be used as a Web form to submit information to a database.

Activating Wizards

Wizards are *add-ins*, which means they do not load by default when Excel loads. You must enable them separately. Most add-ins cause extra commands to appear on the Tools menu, so you can access the add-in programs.

1. **Click** on **Tools**. The Tools menu will appear.

2. **Click** on **Add-Ins**. The Add-Ins dialog box will open.

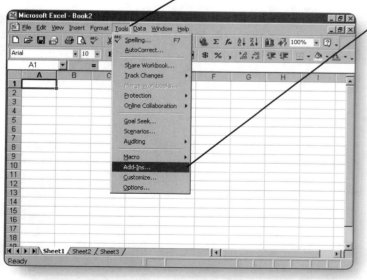

NOTE

If you see a message that the feature is not currently installed, click on Yes to install it.

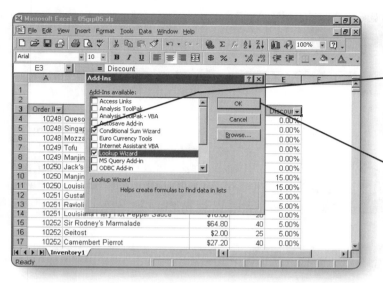

3. Click in the **box** next to each of the add-ins you want to use.

To follow along with the example in this chapter, make sure that you include Conditional Sum Wizard.

4. Click on **OK**. The add-ins you chose will be loaded, and the Add-Ins dialog box will close.

The Conditional Sum Wizard

In this example, you'll learn about the Conditional Sum Wizard. You can use this wizard to add numbers (such as the numbers that represent the value of all HP printers) that meet particular criteria.

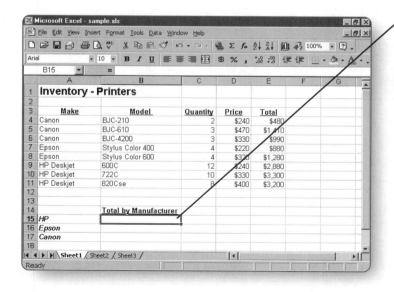

The following steps will insert a formula that calculates the total number of items in the inventory for each manufacturer.

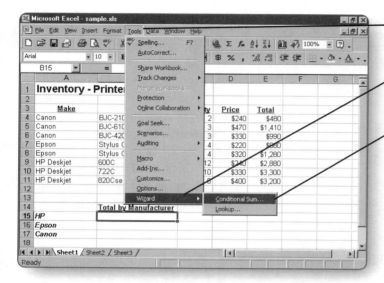

1. Click on **Tools**. The Tools menu will appear.

2. Click on **Wizard**. A submenu will appear.

3. Click on **Conditional Sum**. The Conditional Sum Wizard – Step 1 of 4 dialog box will open. It will ask for a list that "contains the values to sum, including the column labels."

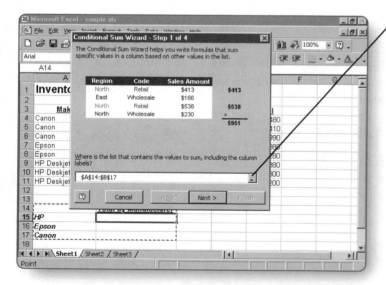

4. Click on the **Collapse Dialog button**. You will return to the worksheet.

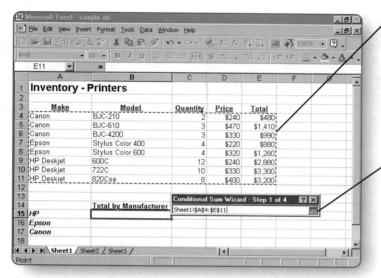

5. **Click** and **drag** the **mouse arrow** across the **range** that contains the data you want to sum. The cells will be highlighted. Don't forget to include the labels at the top of the rows.

6. **Click** on the **Expand Dialog button** to return to the wizard. The Step 1 dialog box will reappear.

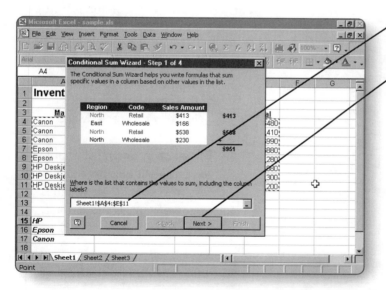

The range you selected will be entered in the dialog box.

7. **Click** on **Next**. The Conditional Sum Wizard – Step 2 of 4 dialog box will open.

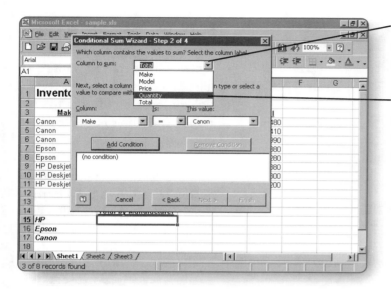

8. Click on the **down arrow** (▼) next to Column to sum:. A drop-down list will appear.

9. Click on the **label** for the column where the numbers you want to add are located, in this case, Quantity.

10. Click on the **down arrow** (▼) next to Column:. A drop-down list will appear.

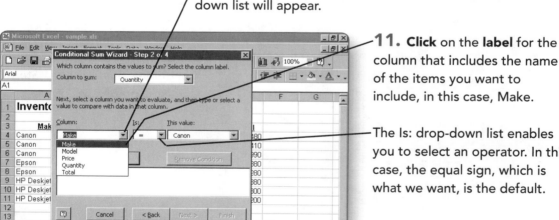

11. Click on the **label** for the column that includes the name of the items you want to include, in this case, Make.

The Is: drop-down list enables you to select an operator. In this case, the equal sign, which is what we want, is the default.

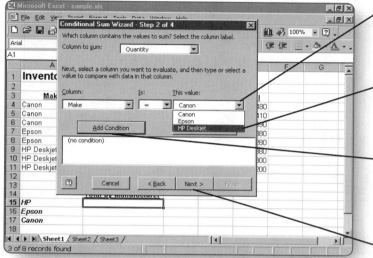

12. **Click** on the **down arrow** (▼) next to This value:. A drop-down list will appear.

13. **Click** on the **label** for the items you want to add, in this case, HP DeskJet.

14. **Click** on **Add Condition** and check that the statement that appears in the text box is what you want to do.

15. **Click** on **Next**. The Conditional Sum Wizard – Step 3 of 4 dialog box will open.

16. **Click** on one of the two copying **options**:

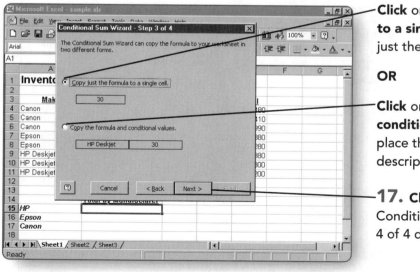

Click on **Copy just the formula to a single cell**. This will place just the result in a cell.

OR

Click on **Copy the formula and conditional values.** This will place the result in a cell and a descriptive label next to it.

17. **Click** on **Next**. The Conditional Sum Wizard – Step 4 of 4 dialog box will open.

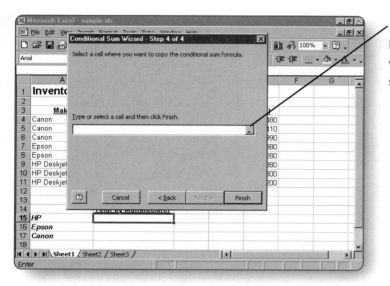

18. **Click** on the **Collapse Dialog button** to return to the worksheet. The dialog box will shrink.

19. **Click** in the **cell** where you want the total to appear. The cell will be highlighted.

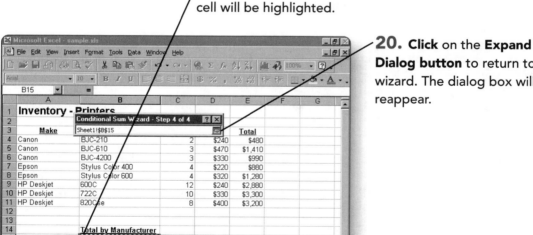

20. **Click** on the **Expand Dialog button** to return to the wizard. The dialog box will reappear.

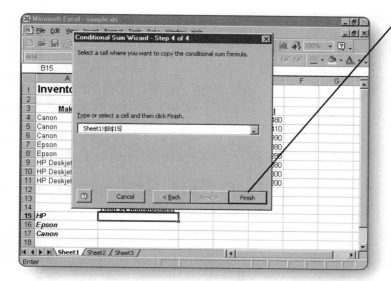

21. Click on **Finish**. The dialog box will close.

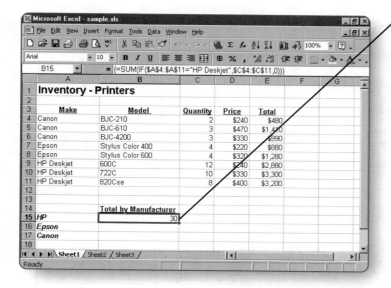

The result will appear in the selected cell.

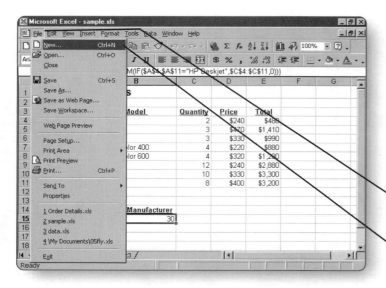

Opening a Template

You learned how to start new documents based on templates earlier in this book, but sometimes you might need to modify the template itself.

1. Click on **File**. The File menu will appear.

2. Click on **New**. The New dialog box will open.

3. Click on the **Spreadsheet Solutions tab**. The tab will come to the front.

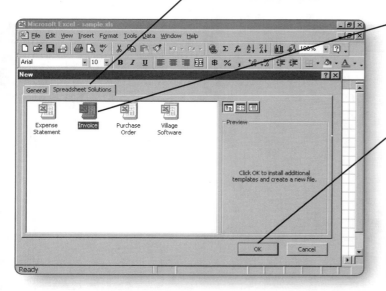

4. Click on the **Invoice icon**. The icon will be highlighted. You will be able to see a small portion of the Invoice template in the Preview box as well.

5. Click on **OK**. The macro warning dialog box will appear.

NOTE

If you have not used the Invoice template before, you may be prompted to insert your Office 2000 CD so that it can be installed. Do so, and click Yes (if prompted) to continue.

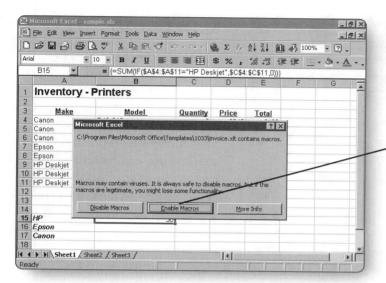

This warning dialog box explains that macros may contain viruses and that you can disable the macros if you're not sure whether the workbook template is from a trusted source.

6. Click on **Enable Macros**. Because this template came with the Excel 2000 software, it should be safe.

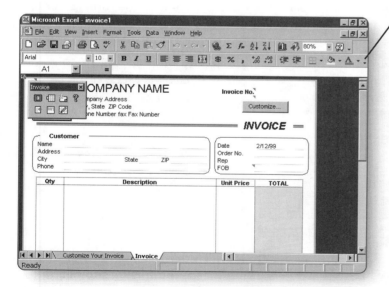

The Invoice template will open. It doesn't look like a worksheet, but it is. It has cells and a Formula bar.

At this point, you can customize the template, print it to fill it out by hand, or fill it out onscreen and print it. The next section explains how to customize the Invoice template.

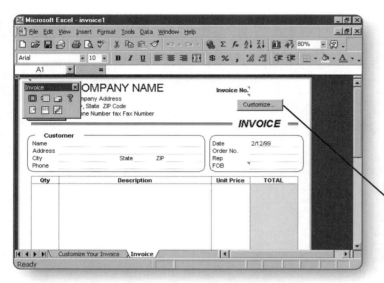

Customizing Your Template

You can add your company name, address, phone number, and so on to your invoice and save it as a new template, which you can use again and again.

1. **Click** on **Customize** to enter your personal information. The Customize Your Invoice worksheet will appear.

You can now replace the boilerplate text in the form. Enter all the information that you want to appear on your invoices such as your company name, address, phone numbers, state and purchase tax rates, credit cards, if appropriate, and shipping charges.

2. **Press** the **Enter key** or **click** in each **text box** to move between entries.

TIP

Move the pointer over the red triangles to get helpful information.

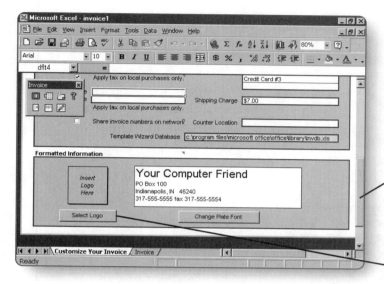

Adding a Logo

Adding a company logo is optional. If you don't want to add a logo, do not perform the following steps. The Insert Logo Here box will not print on your invoice.

1. Scroll to the **bottom** of the **Customize Your Invoice worksheet** to the Formatted Information area.

2. Click on **Select Logo**. The Insert Picture dialog box will open.

3. Locate the **graphic** you want to use. You'll need to look for a folder that contains graphic files. Some clip art files that come with Microsoft Office are probably in C:\Program Files\ Common Files\Microsoft Shared\Clipart. Explore the folders there to find some art you like.

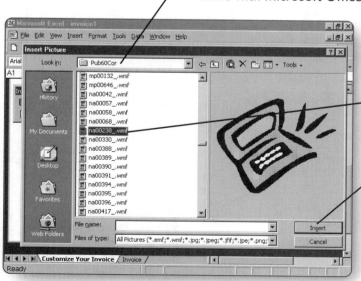

4. Click on the **filename** of the graphic you want to use. The filename will be highlighted.

5. Click on **Insert**. The graphic will be inserted, and the Insert Picture dialog box will close.

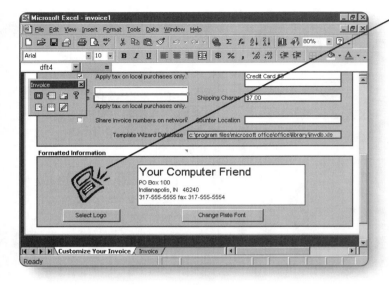

The logo will appear in the Formatted Information box.

The logo and address will appear at the top of all your invoices as if you were using preprinted letterhead.

Saving the Customized Invoice Template

After you've finished customizing your invoice template, you'll want to save it so that you can use it again and again.

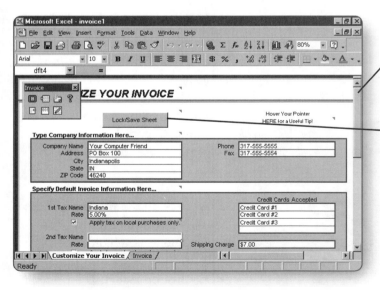

1. Scroll to the **top** of the **Customize Your Invoice worksheet**.

2. Click on the **Lock/Save Sheet button**. The Lock/Save dialog box will open. Lock stops accidental changes from being made to your customized template.

NOTE

The Lock/Save button will change to Unlock after you have locked your template. You can click on this button at a later date to make changes.

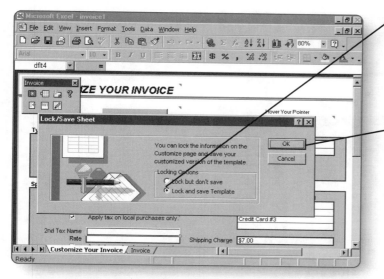

3. Click on **Lock and save Template**. By selecting Lock and save Template, you are creating your own version of the template for future use.

4. Click on **OK**. The Save Template dialog box will open.

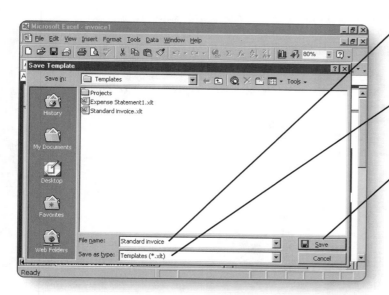

5. Type a **name** for your invoice in the File name: text box.

6. Make sure Templates is selected in the Save as type: text box.

7. Click on **Save**. A message box will open.

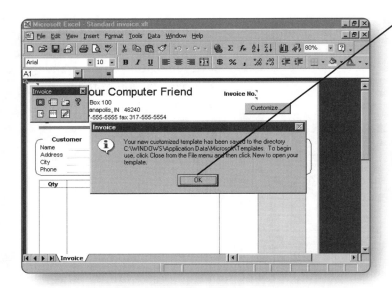

8. Click on **OK**. The new customized template will be saved.

9. Click on **File**. The File menu will appear.

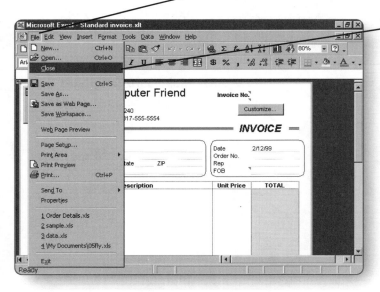

10. Click on **Close**. The template will close, and you are ready to use it to create new workbooks.

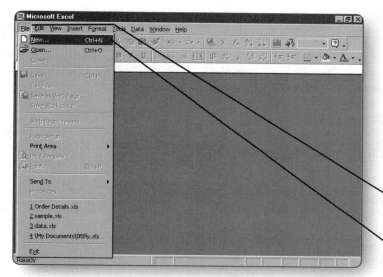

Using a Template

This section shows you how to use a template to create a document. The steps are the same for any template whether it's built-in or a customized template.

1. Click on **File**. The File menu will appear.

2. Click on **New**. The New dialog box will open.

3. Click on the **tab** where the template icon you want to use is located. As a general rule, the built-in templates are on the Spreadsheets Solutions tab, and the custom templates are on the General tab.

4. Click on a **template icon**. The icon will be highlighted.

5. Click on **OK**. The template will appear.

NOTE

If the macro warning message appears again, click on Enable Macros.

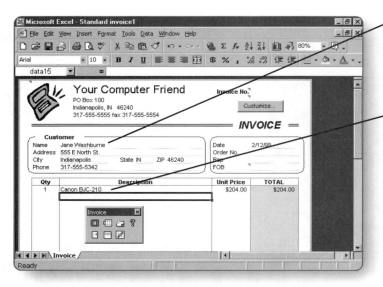

6. **Type** the **information** you want to appear in the template. In this example, you will enter customer information.

7. **Type** the **items** to be invoiced. You may need to scroll down the screen.

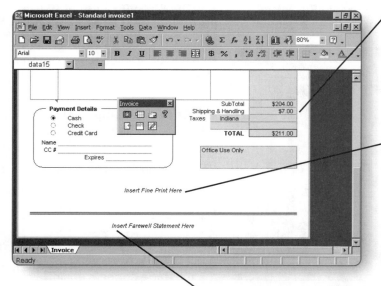

Notice that the template contains the formulas and functions to calculate all the totals including shipping and handling, and taxes. These items are added automatically.

Insert Fine Print Here can be selected and replaced with information for the customer, such as a returns policy or warranties, or it can be deleted by clicking on Edit and then Clear.

Similarly, Insert Farewell Statement Here can be selected and replaced with text such as a company slogan or mission statement, or it can be deleted by clicking on Edit and then Clear.

11

Exploring Print Options

Although you can send your worksheets directly to paper by clicking on File, and then Print, as described in Chapter 3, "Saving, Printing, and Exiting Excel," other options are available. These options not only make your documents look more professional but also save you time and money by letting you see exactly what you're going to print before you use any paper. In this chapter, you'll learn how to:

- Set paper size, paper orientation, and margins
- Add headers and footers
- Select rows and columns to print on every page
- Select the print area
- Set page breaks
- Preview your document

Setting Paper Size and Orientation

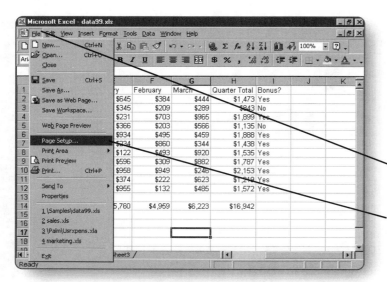

Unlike letters, which are always printed using Portrait orientation, some worksheets may look better printed using Landscape orientation. You'll need to make decisions about how your printouts will look.

1. Click on **File**. The File menu will appear.

2. Click on **Page Setup**. The Page Setup dialog box will open.

3. Click on the **Page tab**. In this tab, you can:

● Select Portrait or Landscape orientation

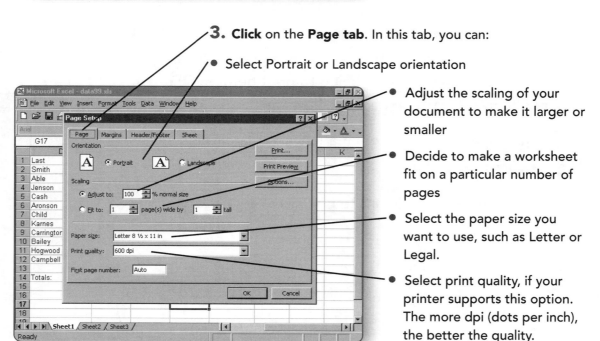

● Adjust the scaling of your document to make it larger or smaller

● Decide to make a worksheet fit on a particular number of pages

● Select the paper size you want to use, such as Letter or Legal.

● Select print quality, if your printer supports this option. The more dpi (dots per inch), the better the quality.

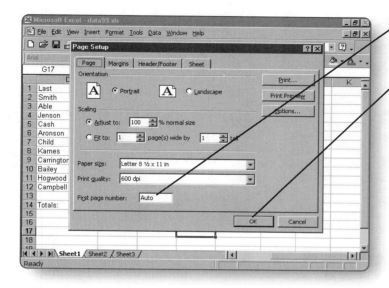

- Select the first page number to print, if you don't want to start at 1.

4a. **Click** on **OK**. Your selections will be saved, and the Page Setup dialog box will close.

OR

4b. **Click** on **another tab** to get more options.

Setting Margins

To adjust your margins, click on File, and then Page Setup to open the Page Setup dialog box, if it's not already open.

1. Click on the **Margins tab**. The tab will come to the front. In this tab, you can:

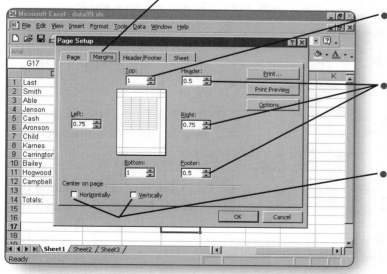

- Adjust the top, bottom, left, and right margins using the up and down arrows (◆).

- Adjust where the header and footer appear on a page by clicking on the up and down arrows (◆).

- Select to center a document either horizontally, vertically, or both.

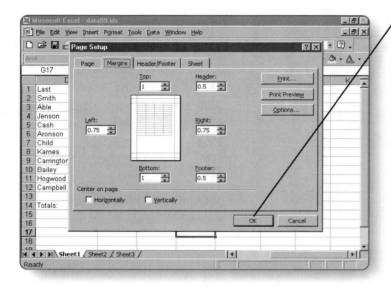

2a. Click on **OK**. Your selections will be saved, and the Page Setup dialog box will close.

OR

2b. Click on **another tab** to get more options.

Adding Headers and Footers

Headers and *footers* are simply text that appears either at the top (header) or bottom (footer) of every page. The types of information typically included in headers and footers are report titles, dates, page numbers, or filenames.

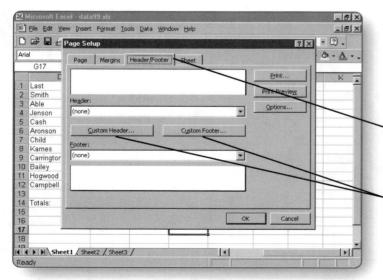

To add headers and footers, click on File, and then Page Setup to open the Page Setup dialog box, if it's not already open.

1. Click on the **Header/Footer tab**. The tab will come to the front.

2. Click on **Custom Header** or **Custom Footer**. The Header or Footer dialog box will open.

3. Click in the **Left**, **Center**, or **Right section text box**. This will determine where the text you insert will appear; left, right, or centered on the printed page.

If desired, click on the A button to open a Font dialog box, where you can change the font for the header or footer. Then click OK to return here.

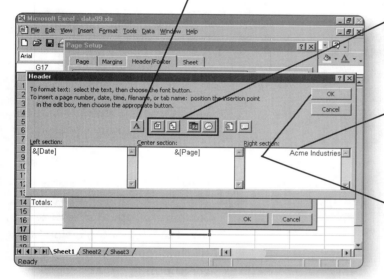

4. Insert a **page number**, **date**, **time**, **filename**, or **tab name** in a text box by clicking on the appropriate button.

5. Type any **text** that you want to appear in the header or footer in the appropriate text box.

6. Click on **OK**. The Header/Footer tab will reappear.

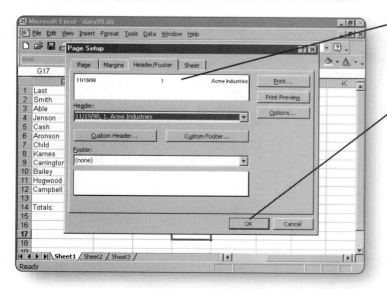

Notice that you will see a preview of how the header or footer will appear in the Header/Footer tab.

7a. Click on **OK**. Your selections will be saved, and the Page Setup dialog box will close.

OR

7b. Click on **another tab** to get more options.

Selecting Rows and Columns to Appear on Every Page

The final tab in the Page Setup dialog box is the Sheet tab. From here, you can make a number of choices including selecting rows or columns, which contain headings or labels, to repeat on every page.

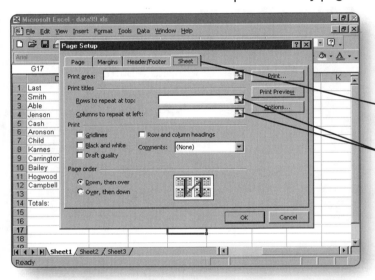

First, click on File, and then Page Setup to open the Page Setup dialog box, if it's not already open.

1. Click on the **Sheet tab**. The tab will come to the front.

2. Click on the **Collapse Dialog button** at the end of either the **Rows to repeat at top: or Columns to repeat at left: text box**. The Page Setup dialog box will shrink to reveal the worksheet.

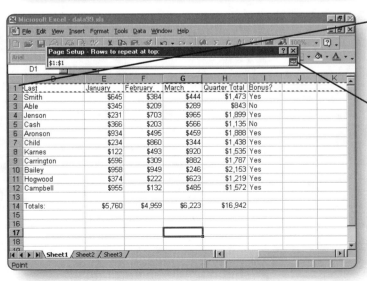

3. Select the **cells** you want to appear on each page. A marquee will appear around the highlighted cells.

4. Click on the **Expand Dialog button**. The Page Setup dialog box will reappear. The range will be automatically entered in the correct Print titles text box.

Other options in the Sheet tab you can select are:

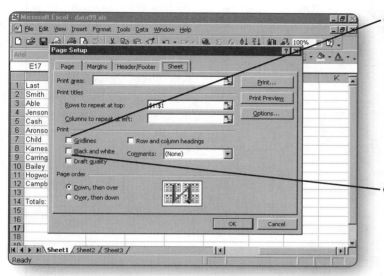

- **Gridlines.** Your printout will have the same grid as your worksheet does on the screen. If you don't select this option, there are no lines separating the rows and columns on the printout, even though you see them on the screen.

- **Black and white.** This will save the ink in your color printing cartridge, if you have one. Color cartridges are usually more expensive than black and white.

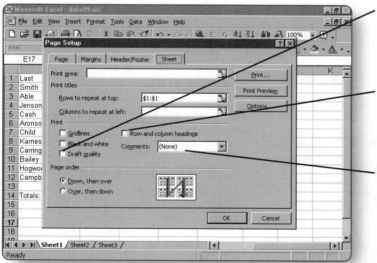

- **Draft quality.** Printing in draft quality is quicker, although the printout will not be quite as sharp.

- **Row and column headings.** Select row and column headings to print column letters and row numbers.

- **Comments.** You can choose to not print your comments by clicking on (None) from the drop-down list. You can also select to either print your comments at the end of the worksheet or as displayed on the sheet.

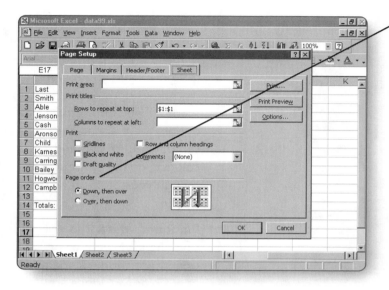

• **Page order.** If your worksheet is both wider and longer than a single page, you can also choose whether to print pages down the worksheet before going across, or whether to go across first and then down.

5a. **Click** on **OK**. Your selections will be saved, and the Page Setup dialog box will close.

OR

5b. **Click** on **another tab** to get more options.

Setting the Print Area

You may not want to print your entire worksheet. For example, you may have 12 months of data in the worksheet and you only want to print the information for the current month.

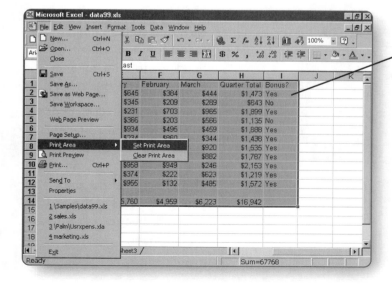

1. **Click** and **drag** with the **mouse arrow** over the area in the worksheet you want to print. The cells will be highlighted.

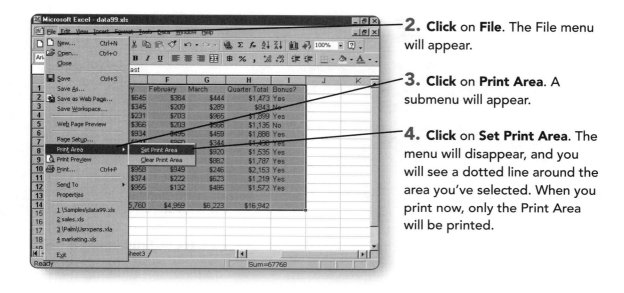

2. Click on **File**. The File menu will appear.

3. Click on **Print Area**. A submenu will appear.

4. Click on **Set Print Area**. The menu will disappear, and you will see a dotted line around the area you've selected. When you print now, only the Print Area will be printed.

Clearing the Print Area

When you clear the print area, the whole sheet becomes re-selected as the print area, so that when you print, the entire sheet prints.

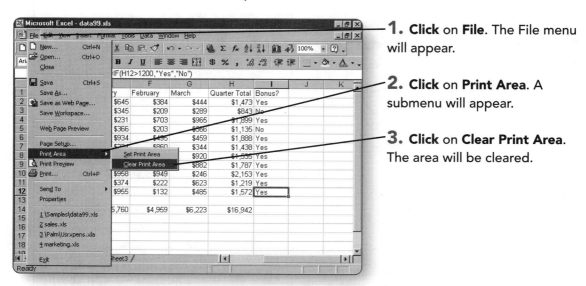

1. Click on **File**. The File menu will appear.

2. Click on **Print Area**. A submenu will appear.

3. Click on **Clear Print Area**. The area will be cleared.

Previewing Your Worksheet

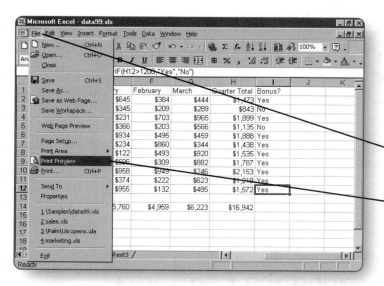

You'll probably save yourself a lot of paper if you always preview your worksheet to see what it looks like and check the margins before sending it to the printer.

1. Click on **File**. The File menu will appear.

2. Click on **Print Preview**. The print preview window will open.

Zooming

Depending on what you are doing, you may find it better to zoom in or out to see more or less of the worksheet at once.

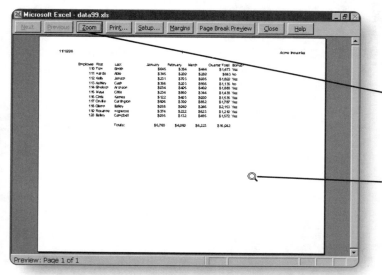

For example, to look at the worksheet as a whole, zoom out; to focus on particular cells, zoom in.

1. Click on the **Zoom button** to zoom to a closer view of your worksheet. The worksheet will be magnified.

Your mouse pointer is a magnifying class while zoomed out in Print Preview. Position it over any area of the worksheet and click to zoom in on that area.

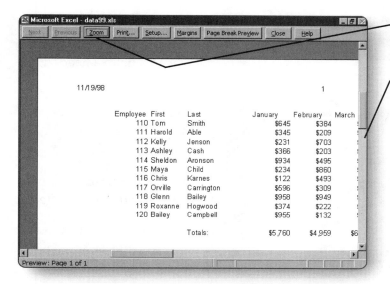

2. Click on **Zoom** again. The worksheet will shrink.

While zoomed in, you can use the scroll bars to view different parts of the worksheet.

Adjusting Margins

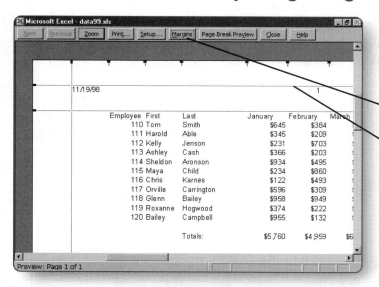

The margin settings control where the worksheet will appear on the printed page. To adjust the margins, follow these steps.

1. Click on the **Margin button**.

The margin settings, columns, and header and footer areas of your worksheet will be revealed.

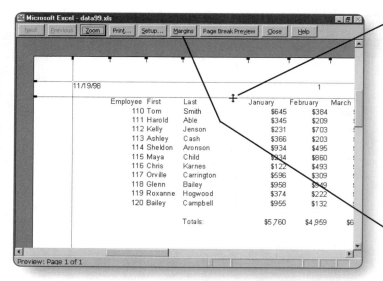

2. **Move** the **mouse arrow** over a margin line until it changes to a double-headed arrow.

3. **Press** and **hold** the **mouse button** as you **drag** the margin in or out, or up or down.

4. **Release** the **mouse button**. The new setting will take effect.

5. **Click** the **Margins button** again. The margin lines will be turned off.

Previewing Page Breaks

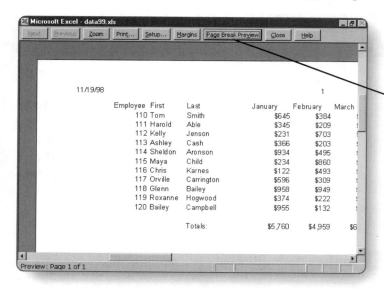

Page Breaks are inserted by Excel to divide large worksheets into pages.

1. **Click** on **Page Break Preview**. The Welcome to Page Break Preview dialog box will open.

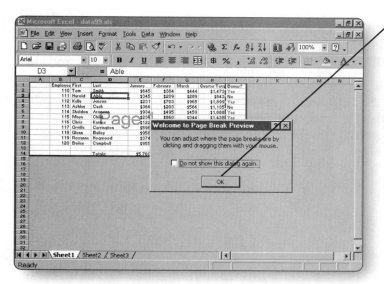

2. Click on **OK**. In the worksheet, you will see where Excel has inserted page breaks either because it knows it can't fit more information on a page or because you selected a particular page range. You can move page breaks, to get a better grouping of rows on pages.

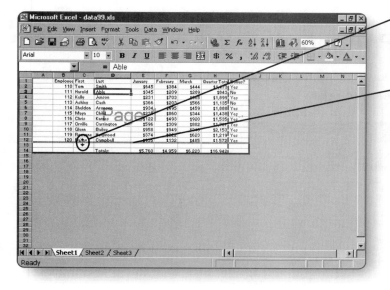

3. Point to a **page break line**. A double-headed arrow will appear.

4. Drag the **page break line** to a new position.

Closing Page Break Preview

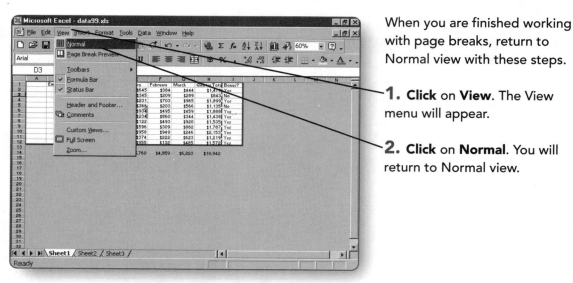

When you are finished working with page breaks, return to Normal view with these steps.

1. Click on **View**. The View menu will appear.

2. Click on **Normal**. You will return to Normal view.

Printing Your Worksheet

Now that you've checked all your printing options, you are ready to print.

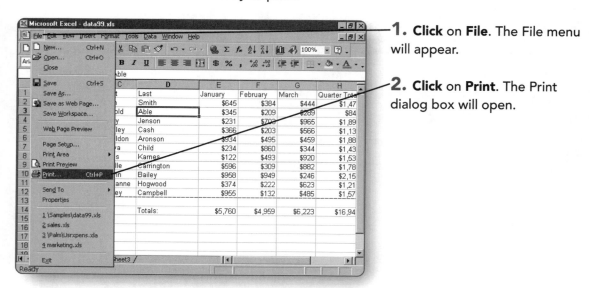

1. Click on **File**. The File menu will appear.

2. Click on **Print**. The Print dialog box will open.

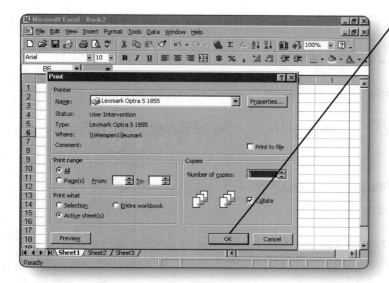

3. Click on **OK**. The document will be printed.

Refer to Chapter 3, "Saving, Printing, and Exiting Excel," for more information about options in the Print dialog box.

Part II Review Questions

1. In Excel, what is a range? *See "Selecting Cells" in Chapter 5*

2. How can you quickly fill a range with a series of data? *See "Filling a Range" in Chapter 5*

3. What role do formulas play in Excel? *See "Entering a Simple Calculation" in Chapter 6*

4. In Excel, what are functions? *See "Using Built-In Functions" in Chapter 6*

5. Why would you want to name a range? *See "Naming a Range" in Chapter 7*

6. Why would you want to split an Excel window? *See "Splitting a Window" in Chapter 7*

7. What is a macro? *See the introduction in Chapter 8*

8. In Excel, how can you sort the data rows in a particular order? *See "Sorting Data" in Chapter 9*

9. In Excel, what are the differences between wizards and templates? *See the introduction in Chapter 10*

10. What feature can you use to see your worksheet before you print it? *See "Previewing Your Worksheet" in Chapter 11*

PART III

Making Your Data Look Good

12

Formatting Text

You can make your worksheets easier to read and more interesting by formatting text effectively. You can use different fonts; change the alignment; add borders, lines, and colors; and more! In this chapter, you'll learn how to:

- Use AutoFormat
- Change the type and size of a font
- Use bold, italic, and underline styles
- Align your text
- Center a heading across your worksheet

Using AutoFormat

If you're not artistically inclined, AutoFormat is a great tool for creating cool worksheets quickly and easily. AutoFormat allows you to choose from a number of professionally designed formats that automatically add colors, fonts, lines, borders, and more to your worksheets.

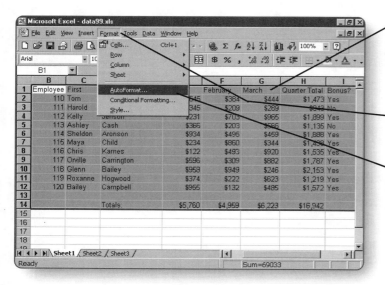

1. Click and **drag** with the **mouse arrow** across the cells you want to format. The cells will be highlighted.

2. Click on **Format**. The Format menu will appear.

3. Click on **AutoFormat**. The AutoFormat dialog box will open.

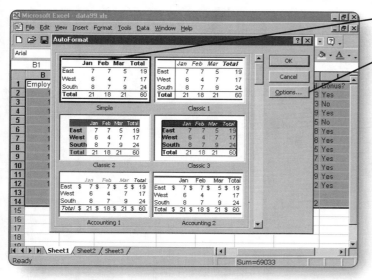

4. Click on a **sample format**.

You can set additional options by clicking on the Options button.

5. Click on **OK** when you find an effect you like. The effect will be applied to the selected cells.

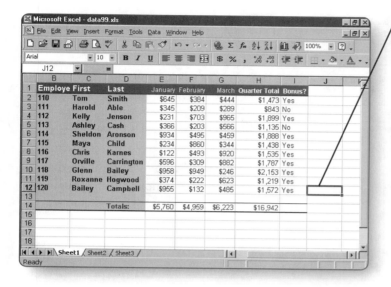

6. Click away from the **cells**. The cells will be deselected, and you will be able to see the full effect of the formatting.

Depending on your selection, AutoFormat may have applied color, changed your fonts, applied italic or bold, and adjusted row heights.

Removing AutoFormat

If you do not like the look that AutoFormat has provided, you can easily remove it.

1. Re-select the **cells** containing the AutoFormatting if they are not selected. The cells will be highlighted.

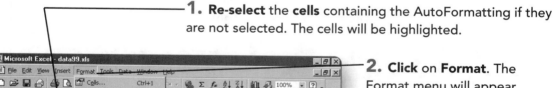

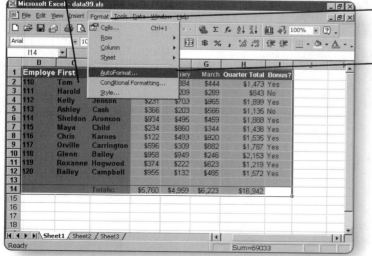

2. Click on **Format**. The Format menu will appear.

3. Click on **AutoFormat**. The AutoFormat dialog box will open.

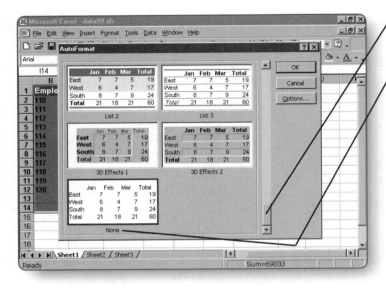

4. Scroll to the **bottom** of the AutoFormats.

5. Click on **None** from the list of formats. (It's all the way at the bottom of the list.) The selection will be highlighted.

6. Click on **OK**. AutoFormat will be removed from your worksheet.

Using Fonts

Fonts are typefaces in different styles and sizes that give your text character and impact.

1. Select the **cell(s)** containing the text you want to format. The cell(s) will be highlighted.

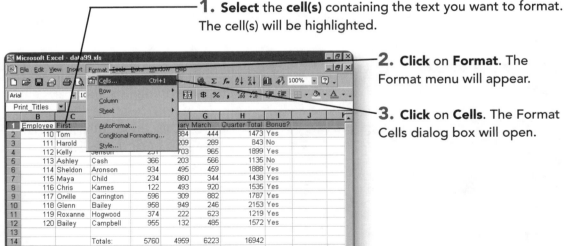

2. Click on **Format**. The Format menu will appear.

3. Click on **Cells**. The Format Cells dialog box will open.

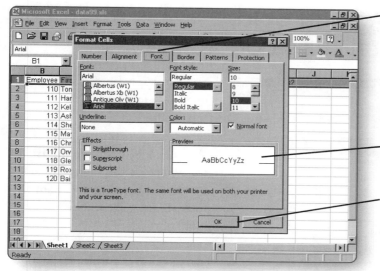

4. Click on the **Font tab**. In this tab, you can select:

- A Font, Font style, and Size from the drop-down lists.

- Underline, Color, and Effects.

As you make your selections, you can preview the results.

5. Click on **OK**, when you're happy with the preview.

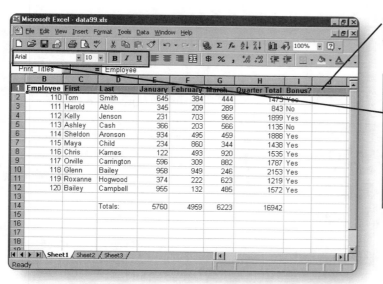

Your selections will be applied to the text.

NOTE

You can also change the font, font size, font color, and other attributes using the Formatting toolbar controls.

Adding Bold, Italic, and Underline

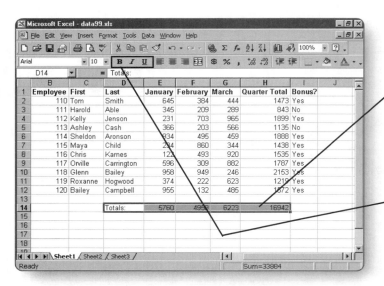

You can apply bold, italic, and underline formatting from the toolbar.

1. **Click** and **drag** the **mouse arrow** across the range of cells containing the text you want to format. The cells will be highlighted.

2. **Click** on the **Bold**, **Italic,** or **Underline buttons**. The effect(s) will be immediately applied to your text.

NOTE

You can select more than one attribute at a time. To remove an effect, select the text and click on the respective style button.

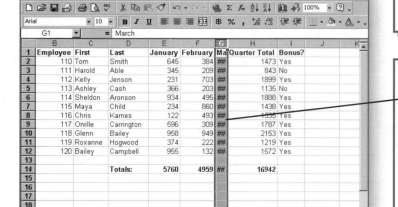

TIP

If the numbers become # symbols, the new font has made the text too wide to fit in the column. See Chapter 5, "Editing Worksheets," for information on adjusting column widths.

Aligning Your Text

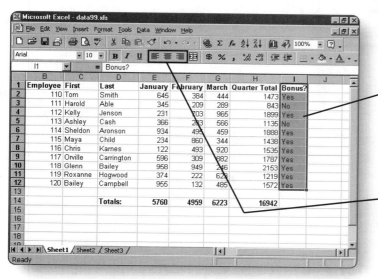

You can make a worksheet easier to read by aligning the text appropriately.

1. Click and **drag** the **mouse arrow** across the range of cells with the text that needs to be aligned. The cells will be highlighted.

2. Click on the **Left**, **Center**, or **Right align buttons**. The text will be aligned. In this example, the text has been left aligned.

Centering a Heading Over More Than One Column

If you want to center a heading over more than one column, use the Merge and Center button.

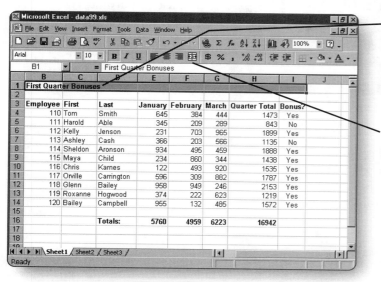

1. Click and **drag** with the **mouse arrow** across the range of cells that need to have centered text. The cells will be highlighted.

2. Click on the **Merge** and **Center button**. The cells will be centered in one large cell.

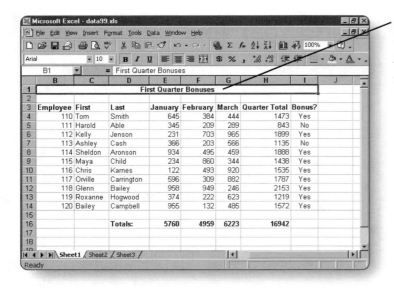

In this example, eight cells have been merged into one large cell, A1. The text has also been centered.

Other Alignment Options

You can also merge cells, wrap text in a cell, vertically align, shrink text to fit, and rotate text.

1. Click and **drag** the **mouse arrow** across the range that contains the text you want to format. The cells will be highlighted.

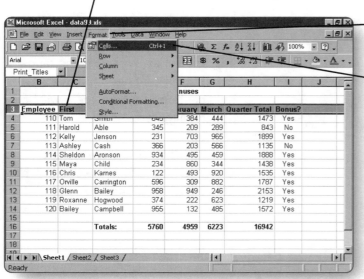

2. Click on **Format**. The Format menu will appear.

3. Click on **Cells**. The Format Cells dialog box will open.

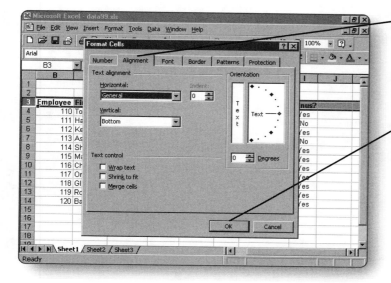

4. **Click** on the **Alignment tab**. The tab will come to the front.

5. **Click** on whatever **option** you want to select and change.

6. **Click** on **OK**. The change(s) you made will be applied.

13

Formatting Numbers and Cells

The numbers you enter in a worksheet represent many values, such as dollars and cents, percentages, and dates. You need to format your raw numbers so that they're easy to recognize. You can also draw attention to particular cells with color, shading, and borders. In this chapter, you'll learn how to:

- Add dollar signs and decimal places
- Format percentages
- Insert today's date and select a date format
- Add total lines and borders
- Apply color backgrounds and patterns

Formatting Currency and Percentages

Dollar and percentage signs enable you to quickly recognize numerical amounts in a worksheet.

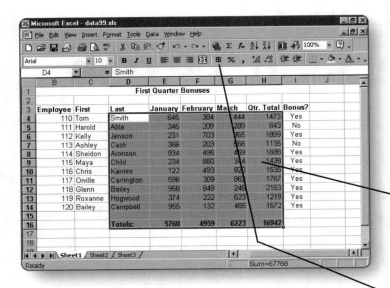

Formatting Currency

When you format text as currency, a currency symbol appears to its left (usually a $ sign, unless you have set up Excel for a foreign currency), and two decimal places appear in the number.

1. Click and **drag** with the **mouse arrow** across the range that contains or will contain currency. The cells will be highlighted.

2. Click on the **Currency Style button**. The selection will be formatted.

Excel will add a dollar sign, a decimal point, and cents to each entry in the selected range.

If # marks appear in a cell, widen the column, as you learned in Chapter 5, "Editing Worksheets."

Formatting Percentages

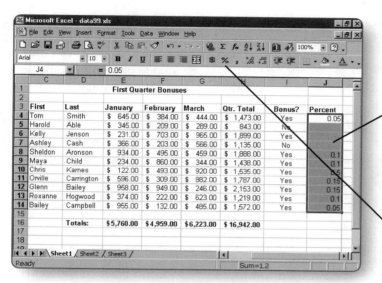

The procedure for formatting numbers to be displayed as percentages is almost exactly the same as for currency.

1. Click and **drag** with the **mouse arrow** across the range containing the data that you want to format as percentages. The cells will be highlighted.

2. Click on the **Percent Style button**. The selection will be formatted.

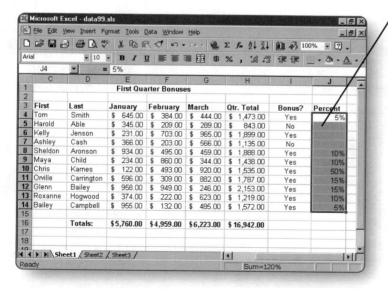

Percentages are much easier to read after they've been formatted. The numbers are rounded, and the percent sign added. Any decimal values not displayed are still used in all calculations.

Adding and Removing Decimal Places

Amounts formatted to currency have two decimal places added for the cents. Percentages are rounded to a whole number. In either case, you may want to hide or display numbers after the decimal point.

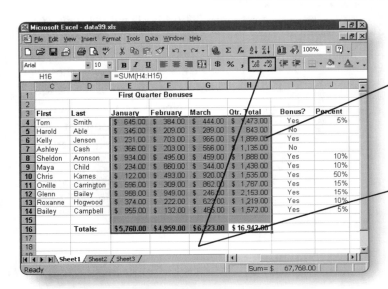

1. Click and **drag** with the **mouse arrow** across the range of cells that contain the numbers you want to format. The cells will be highlighted.

2. Click twice on either the **Increase** or **Decrease Decimal buttons**. The decimal places will increase or disappear.

In this example, after clicking twice on the Decrease Decimal button, two decimal places have disappeared.

NOTE

Even if you display numbers with decimal values as whole numbers, the numbers after the decimal point are still used in all calculations.

Formatting Dates

When you enter numbers for a date into a cell, Excel formats it as MM/DD/YY. You can also have the date appear in a different format.

1. Select the **cell** or the **range** containing the date(s). The cell(s) will be highlighted.

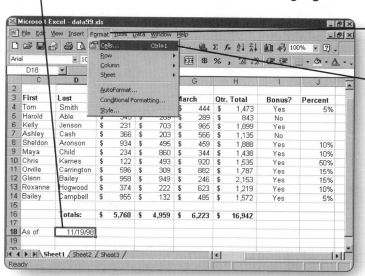

2. Click on **Format**. The Format menu will appear.

3. Click on **Cells**. The Format Cells dialog box will open.

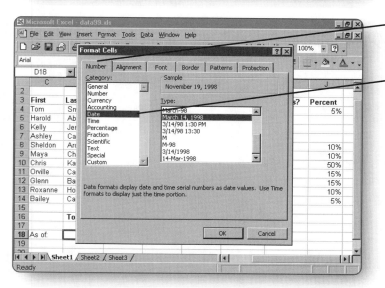

4. Click on the **Number tab**. The tab will come to the front.

5. Click on **Date** in the Category: list. The item will be highlighted.

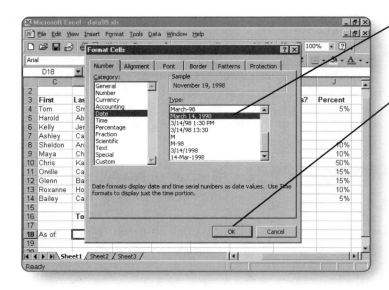

6. **Click** on a **format** in the Type: list. A preview will appear in the Sample area.

7. **Click** on **OK**. The Format Cells dialog box will close.

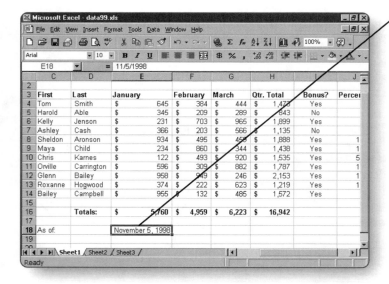

The new format for the date will appear in the cell.

As always, if # marks appear, widen the column, as you learned in Chapter 5.

Inserting Today's Date

You can insert today's date in your worksheet so that every time you open the worksheet the date will be updated. Today's date will also always appear on your printouts, so that if you have many different printouts of the same worksheet, you can easily see which is the most recent version.

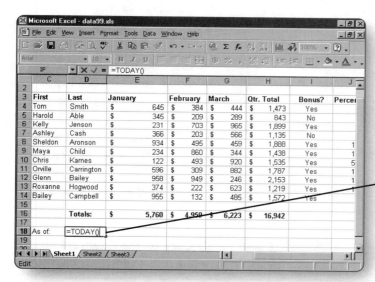

TIP

Double-click on the Clock icon in the right corner of your Windows Taskbar to display or change the date or time on your PC's clock.

1. Click on the **cell** where you want the date to appear. The cell will be highlighted.

2. Type =TODAY().

3. Press the **Enter** key. Today's date will appear in the cell.

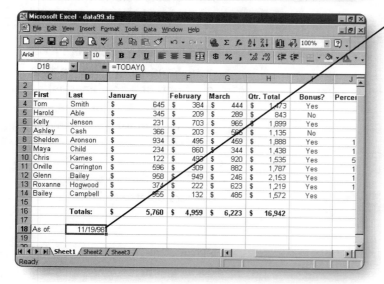

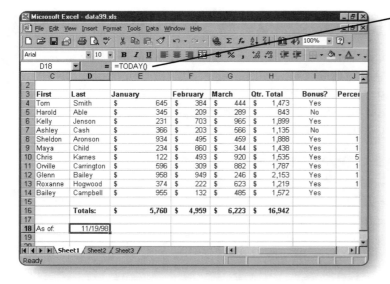

The function, =TODAY(), appears in the formula bar when that cell is selected.

Applying Borders and Total Lines

You can add borders (lines) to individual cells and groups of cells. A border can appear around all sides, or only certain sides (for example, only the bottom of the selected area).

1. Select the **cell** or **range** of cells around which to put a border. The cell(s) will be highlighted.

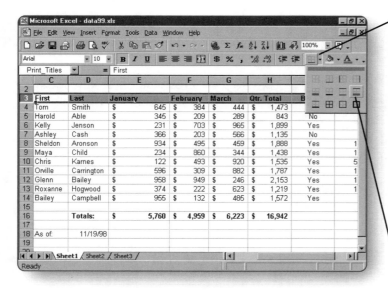

2. Click on the **down arrow** (▼) next to the Borders button. The Borders palette will appear.

Icons displaying how the borders will be applied to a cell or selected range (top, bottom, left, right, or a combination) and the weight of the line (thin, thick, or double) are displayed in the palette.

3. Click on your **selection**. The Borders palette will close.

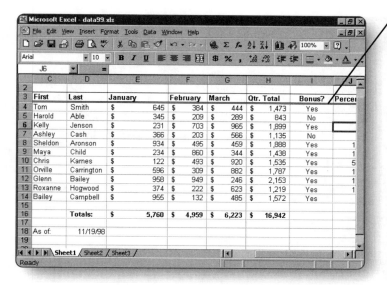

When you deselect the cell or range, you will see the border that you added.

Applying Color and Patterns

If you have a color printer or you want to improve the look of your worksheet on your computer screen, you can add background colors. If you use a black-and-white printer, you can add shades of gray and patterns instead.

Adding a Background Color

Adding a background color can dress up a worksheet by making it more interesting-looking. Be careful, however, that the background you choose does not interfere with the readability of your data.

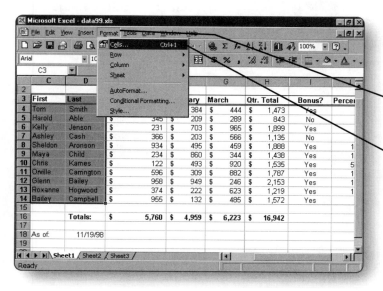

1. **Select** the **cell** or **range** of cells you want to color. The cells will be highlighted.

2. **Click** on **Format**. The Format menu will appear.

3. **Click** on **Cells**. The Format Cells dialog box will open.

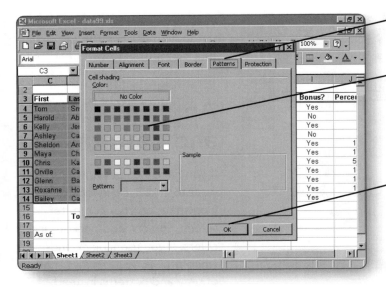

4. Click on the **Patterns tab**. The tab will come to the front.

5. Click on a **color** under the Color: heading. The color box will be highlighted, and a preview will appear in the Sample box.

6. Click on **OK**. The color will be applied to the highlighted cells.

Adding a Pattern

You can use a pattern instead of a color as a background to your cells. A pattern uses two colors, arranged in some design, such as stripes or dots. Each pattern has both a background and a foreground color. The background color is the "base" color, whereas the foreground color is the color of the stripes or dots.

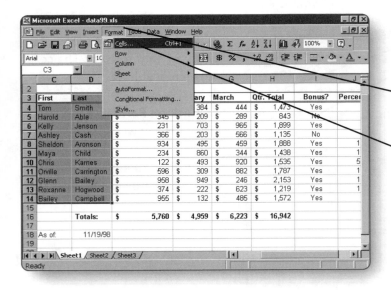

1. Select the **cell** or **range** of cells. The cells will be highlighted.

2. Click on **Format**. The Format menu will appear.

3. Click on **Cells**. The Format Cells dialog box will open.

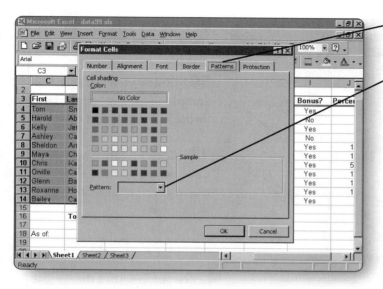

4. Click on the **Patterns tab**. The tab will come to the front.

5. Click on the **down arrow** (▼) next to Pattern: to open the Pattern drop-down list. A palette of patterns and colors will appear.

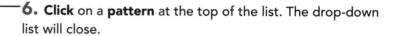

6. Click on a **pattern** at the top of the list. The drop-down list will close.

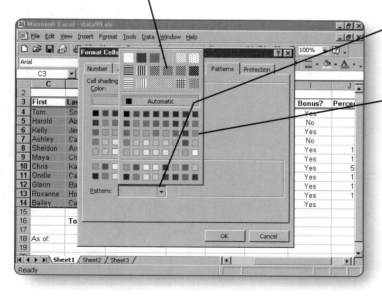

7. Click on the **down arrow** (▼) next to Pattern: again. The drop-down list will appear.

8. Click on a **foreground color** to use. The list will close again.

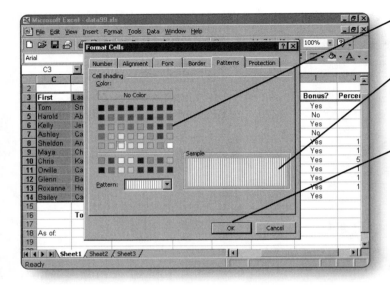

9. Click on a **background color** to use with this pattern.

10. Check your work in the **Sample** area, and repeat steps 2 through 7 as needed.

11. Click on **OK**. The Format Cells dialog box will close. Your changes will appear in the worksheet.

TIP

Remember that the pattern is a background, and if you will be entering data into the cells in the selected range, you need to select a light pattern, so that the data can still be read.

14

Adding Clip Art and WordArt to a Worksheet

Whether you need to make a presentation of financial information to the Board of Directors or PTA, you can add interest and flair to your document with pictures and WordArt. In this chapter, you'll learn how to:

- Add clip art and adjust its size and placement
- Remove the border from clip art and make the background transparent
- Adjust the contrast and brightness of clip art
- Add and edit WordArt

Adding Clip Art

Clip art is a graphic or drawing file that has been created for you to use. By using clip art, you can quickly and easily add illustrations to your document.

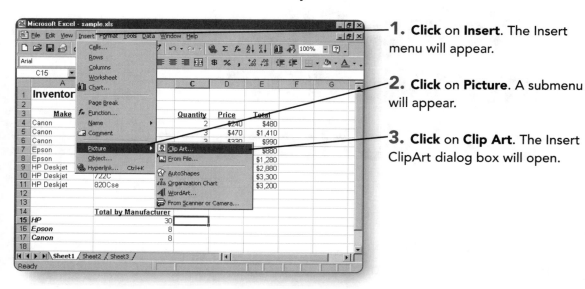

1. Click on **Insert**. The Insert menu will appear.

2. Click on **Picture**. A submenu will appear.

3. Click on **Clip Art**. The Insert ClipArt dialog box will open.

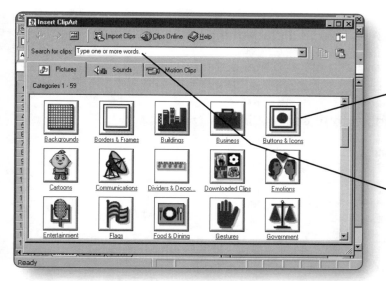

4. Drag the **scroll bar** to scroll through the list of categories to find the one you want.

5a. Click on a **category**. The clips in that category will appear.

OR

5b. Type a **word** that describes the clip you want, such as Printer, in the Search for clips: box, and then press Enter. Clips that match that keyword will appear.

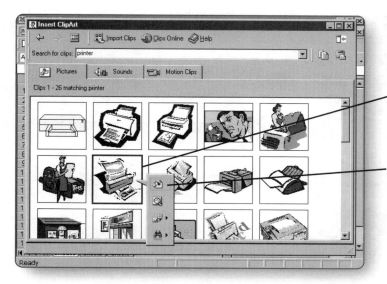

6. Drag the **scroll bar** to scroll through the clips to find the one you want.

7. Click on a **clip art image**. A menu of four buttons will appear.

8. Click on the **Insert Clip** button. The clip art will be placed on top of your worksheet.

9. Click on the **Close button** (⊠). The Insert ClipArt dialog box will close.

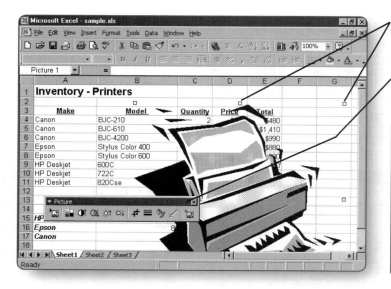

Selection handles will be visible around the box.

The picture toolbar will also open.

TIP

If you decide you don't like the image you inserted, press the Delete key when the clip is selected. The clip will disappear.

Adjusting the Size and Location of Clip Art

Whenever you use clip art, you will need to adjust its size and location so that it fits appropriately with your data. The graphic needs to be big enough to be interesting but not so large that it detracts from the data.

Adjusting the Size of Clip Art

The clip art that comes with Office may not be exactly the size you need for a particular spot. Luckily, you can easily resize any piece to fit your needs.

1. **Move** the **mouse arrow** over one of the selection handles. The arrow will change to a double-headed arrow.

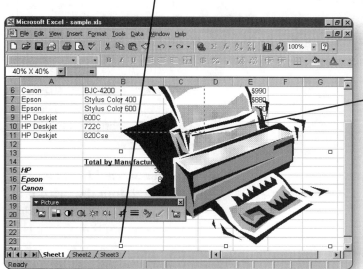

2. **Press** and **hold** the **mouse button** until the pointer changes to a crosshair.

3. **Drag** the **selection handle** in or out. A dotted outline will show where it is going.

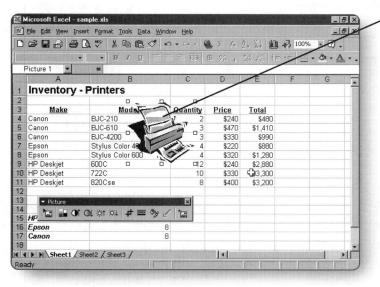

4. **Release** the **mouse button**. The picture will shrink or expand, depending on which way you drag.

TIP

Dragging a corner selection handle sizes a clip art image proportionally. Dragging a top or side handle increases the width or height only, distorting the image.

Moving the Clip Art Image

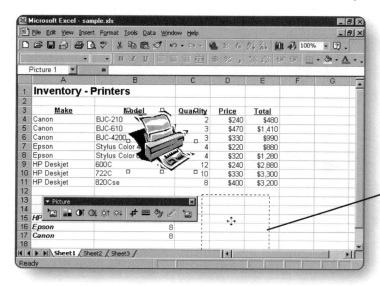

After you have placed a piece of clip art and resized it as needed, you may want to reposition it on the page.

1. Move the **mouse arrow** over the picture. The mouse pointer will change to a four-headed arrow.

2. Press and **hold** the **mouse button** and **drag** the **picture** to a new location. A dotted outline will show where the picture is going.

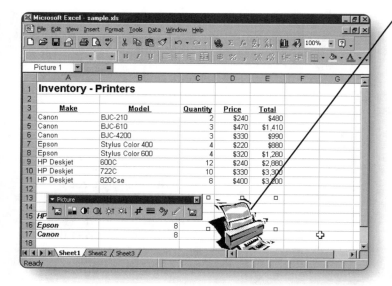

3. Release the **mouse button**. The clip art will be moved.

TIP

When you finally decide where the clip art image looks best, you may find you need to move your data so that it isn't obscured. This is easy. You can use the cut and paste commands covered in Chapter 5, "Editing Worksheets," or you can insert some blank columns or rows (see Chapter 4, "Managing Workbooks and Worksheets").

NOTE

If the Picture toolbar does not appear, open the View menu, point to Toolbars, and click on Picture.

Adjusting the Quality of the Picture

Using the Picture toolbar, you can make adjustments to the picture after you've inserted it.

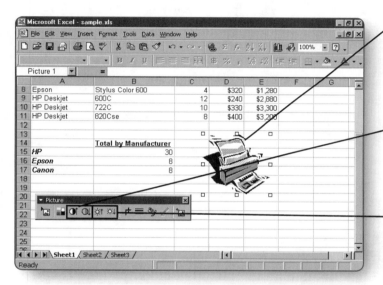

1. **Click** on the **clip art** or other picture that you have inserted. The selection handles will appear, as well as the Picture toolbar.

2. **Click** on the **More Contrast** or **Less Contrast button**. The contrast in the picture will increase or decrease.

3. **Click** on the **More Brightness** or **Less Brightness button**. The brightness in the picture will increase or decrease.

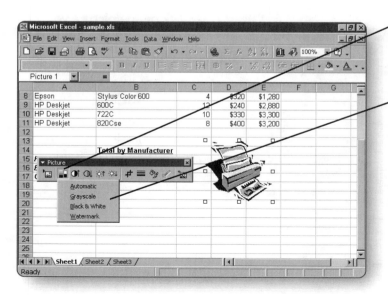

4. **Click** on the **Image Control** button. A list of image types will appear.

5. **Click** on the **image type** you want. If you are not sure, try each type in turn. Automatic is color; Grayscale is a shaded black and white version. Black & White contains no shading. Watermark is a pale ghost of the color image.

Inserting a Picture from a File

In addition to using the clip art provided with Excel, you may want to insert your own pictures that you have scanned or acquired elsewhere.

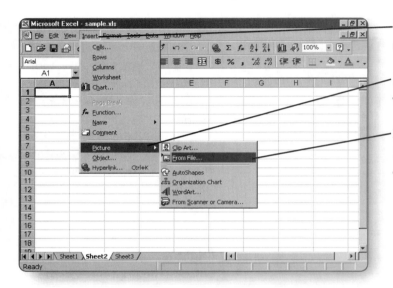

1. **Click** on **Insert**. The Insert menu will appear.

2. **Click** on **Picture**. A submenu will appear.

3. **Click** on **From File**. The Insert Picture dialog box will open.

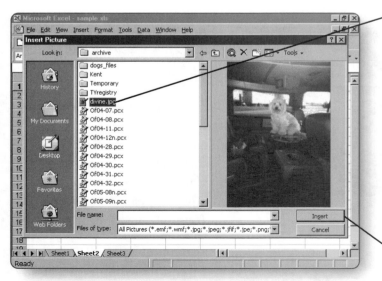

4. **Click** on the **picture** you want to insert. A preview of it will appear.

NOTE

You may need to change the folder using the Look in: drop-down list. Refer back to Chapter 4 if you need help with this.

5. **Click** on **Insert**. The picture will be inserted in your worksheet.

Cropping an Image

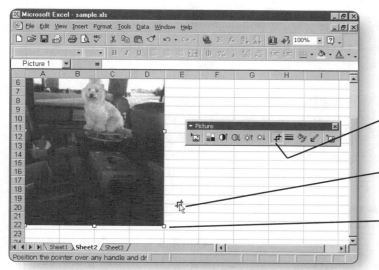

Excel provides a cropping tool that lets you trim extraneous detail from one or more sides of a picture. This works with both clip art and other images.

1. Click on the **Crop button** on the Picture toolbar.

The mouse arrow will change to the cropping tool.

2. Point the **mouse** at a selection handle in a corner that you want to crop out.

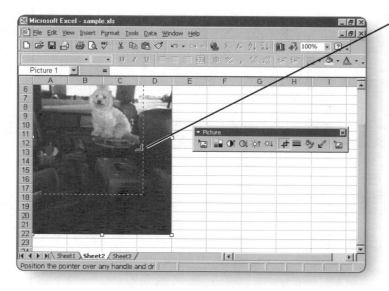

3. Press and **hold** the **mouse button** and **drag** the **crosshair** in toward the center of the picture. A dotted line will show where it is cropping.

4. Release the **mouse button**. The clip art will be adjusted to the new size.

5. Repeat steps 2 through **4**, dragging different selection handles around the image, until it is cropped to your satisfaction.

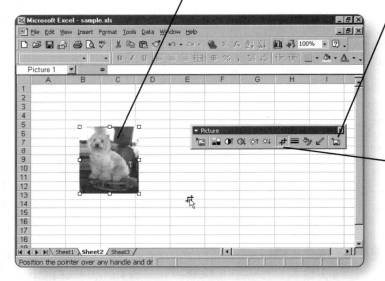

If you crop too much, click on the Reset Picture button, and the cropping will be removed. This button also returns color, brightness, and contrast changes to their original settings.

6. Click on the **Crop** button again. The cropping tool will be deselected.

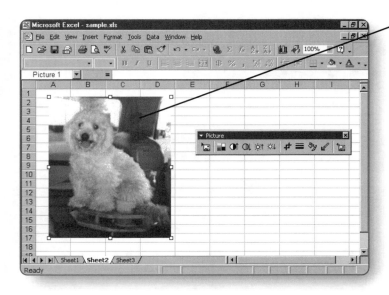

If you want, you can resize the picture and reposition it, as you learned earlier in this chapter.

Adding WordArt

Fonts can add some interest to your text, but for a more dramatic effect try using WordArt. You can apply amazing color schemes, add 3-D effects, and sculpt your words into various shapes.

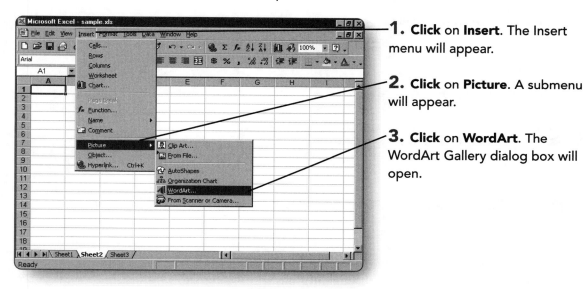

1. Click on **Insert**. The Insert menu will appear.

2. Click on **Picture**. A submenu will appear.

3. Click on **WordArt**. The WordArt Gallery dialog box will open.

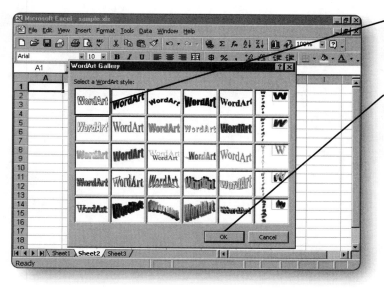

4. Click on a **style** in the WordArt Gallery. A border will appear around your selection.

5. Click on **OK**. The Edit WordArt Text dialog box will open.

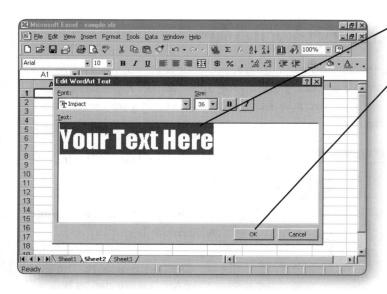

6. Type in **text** to replace "Your Text Here."

7. Click on **OK**. The Edit WordArt Text dialog box will close.

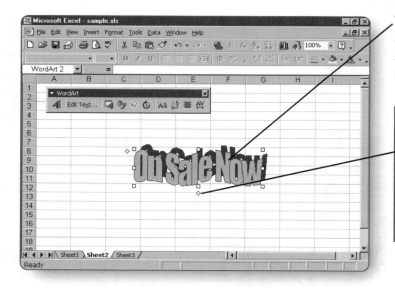

The text will appear in a layer above your worksheet surrounded by selection handles.

TIP

Try dragging the yellow diamonds (there may be only one, depending on the image you chose) to change the perspective.

Changing the Look of Your WordArt

You can move and resize WordArt just as you learned to do with clip art earlier in the chapter. You can also make many adjustments to WordArt from the WordArt toolbar.

Rotating WordArt

Part of the fun of WordArt is that it isn't limited to straight horizontal orientation. You can rotate it a little—or a lot.

1. Click on the **Free Rotate button**. The selection handles will change to green circles.

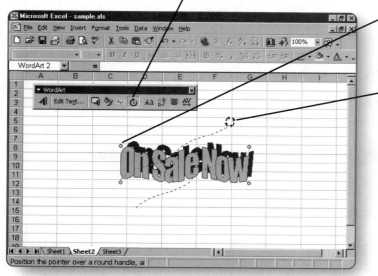

2. Move the **mouse arrow** over one of the selection handles.

3. Click and **drag** the WordArt to a new angle.

4. Click on the **Free Rotate button** again. The feature will be turned off.

Changing the WordArt Shape

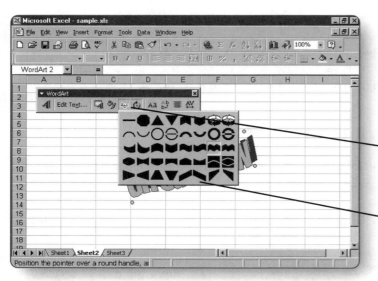

The shape of the WordArt is the curve, line, or solid shape to which it conforms. Each WordArt style has a default shape, but you can change it easily.

1. Click on the **WordArt Shape button**. A palette will appear.

2. Click on a **different shape** for the letters to follow. The WordArt changes to conform to the new shape.

Editing WordArt Text

If you want to change the WordArt text, you do not have to re-create it; simply edit the text as described here.

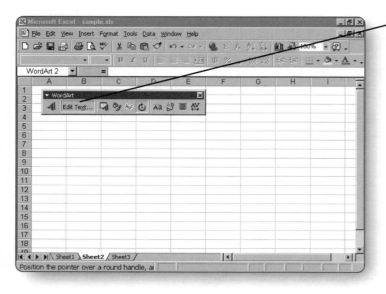

1. Click on the **Edit Text button** to correct typing errors or make changes to the text. The Edit WordArt Text dialog box will open.

2. Make your **changes.**

3. Click on **OK**. Your changes will appear in the document.

TIP

You can do even more with WordArt editing! Try out the four buttons on the right end of the WordArt toolbar, which control the way the text is sized, aligned, and spaced. You can also drag the yellow diamond(s) on the WordArt to change the perspective. Use Ctrl+Z to undo if you make a mistake.

Part III Review Questions

1. Why would you want to use the Excel AutoFormat feature? *See "Using AutoFormat" in Chapter 12*

2. Why does Excel sometimes replace your entries with # signs when you change the font or font size? *See "Using Fonts" in Chapter 12*

3. How can you center a head over more than one column? *See "Centering a Heading Over More Than One Column" in Chapter 12*

4. Why do you need to format numbers? *See the introduction in Chapter 13*

5. How can you quickly format numbers in a cell as dollars and cents? *See "Formatting Currency" in Chapter 13*

6. What do the Increase and Decrease Decimal buttons do in Excel? *See "Adding and Removing Decimal Places" in Chapter 13*

7. How can you add the current date to your worksheet? *See "Inserting Today's Date" in Chapter 13*

8. What is the difference between clip art and WordArt? *See the introduction in Chapter 14*

9. What menu do you use to add clip art or WordArt to an Excel worksheet? *See the introduction in Chapter 14*

10. How can you move or resize clip art after you've added it to a worksheet? *See "Adjusting the Size of Clip Art" in Chapter 14*

PART IV

Creating Charts and Maps of Your Data

15

Generating a Chart

If you've ever spent hours creating charts on graph paper, you'll really appreciate how easy creating a chart is in Excel. Just make a few choices, and you will see your data transformed into a 3-D pie chart complete with data labels. In this chapter, you'll learn how to:

- Use the Chart Wizard to create a chart
- Change the chart type
- Change the way the data is plotted

Creating a Chart with the Chart Wizard

The Chart Wizard is really amazing. It enables you to create a sophisticated chart of your data in just a few minutes.

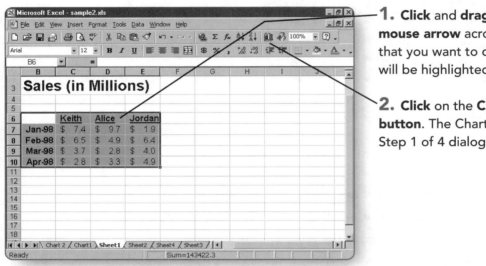

1. Click and **drag** with the **mouse arrow** across the range that you want to chart. The cells will be highlighted.

2. Click on the **Chart Wizard button**. The Chart Wizard – Step 1 of 4 dialog box will open.

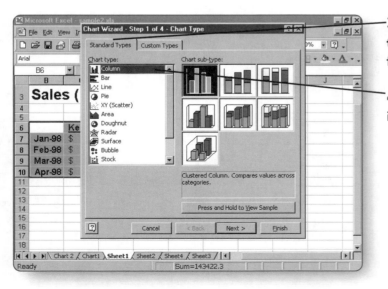

3. Click on the **Standard Types tab**. The tab will come to the front.

4. Click on a **chart type**. The item will be highlighted.

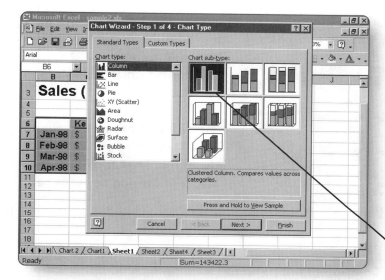

TIP

You can choose any chart type, but if you have more than one data series (that is, multiple rows and multiple columns in your range), don't choose a Pie. Pie charts plot only a single row or a single column of figures.

5. **Click** on an **option** in the Chart sub-type: area. The item will be highlighted.

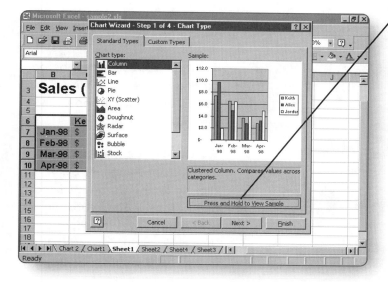

6. **Click** and **hold down** the **mouse button** on the Press and Hold to View Sample button. You will be able to see what your data will look like if you choose a particular chart type. Release the mouse button when you're finished looking.

(Optional) As an alternative to selecting a standard chart type, you can also click on the Custom Types tab. You can choose from charts that have the background, colors, and fonts preselected.

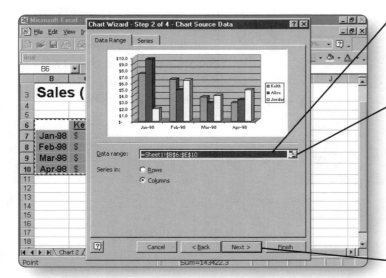

7. **Click** on **Next** after choosing either a standard or custom chart type. The Chart Wizard – Step 2 of 4 dialog box will open.

If you selected your data before clicking on the Chart Wizard in step 2, the data will appear in the Data range: box.

You can change the data by typing a new range, or by clicking on the Collapse Dialog button for the dialog box. Select the range in the worksheet and then click on the Expand Dialog button for the dialog box to return to the wizard.

8. **Click** on **Next**. The Chart Wizard – Step 3 of 4 dialog box will open.

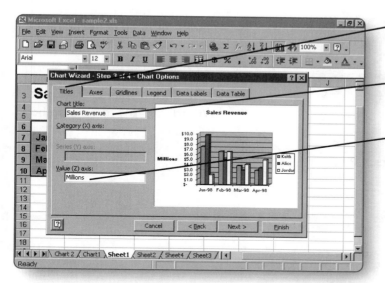

9. Click on the **Titles tab**. The tab will come to the front.

10. Type a **title** for your chart in the Chart title: text box.

11. (Optional) **Type titles** for the X and/or Y axes if you think it will be helpful.

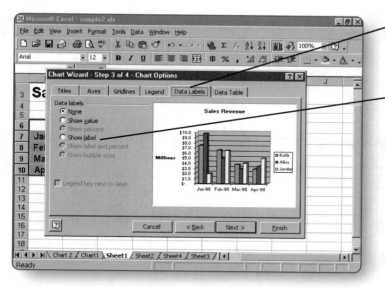

12. Click on the **Data Labels tab**. The tab will come to the front.

13a. Click on **one** of the **Data labels options**. For example, you can choose to display the actual numerical value for each bar, column, or other shape. Or, in a pie chart, you can choose to show the percentage of the whole for each pie wedge.

OR

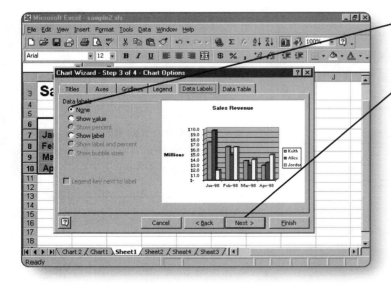

13b. **Click** on **None** in the Data labels box, if you want no options to be applied.

14. **Click** on **Next**. The Chart Wizard – Step 4 of 4 dialog box will open.

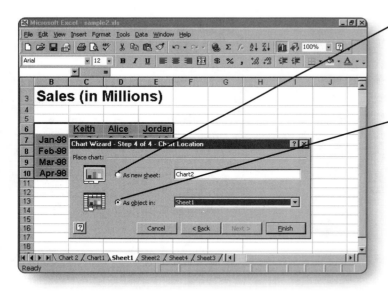

15a. **Click** on **As new sheet:** to create your chart on a new worksheet.

OR

15b. **Click** on **As object in:** to add it to the worksheet that contains the data, so that you can print both the data and the chart on the same page.

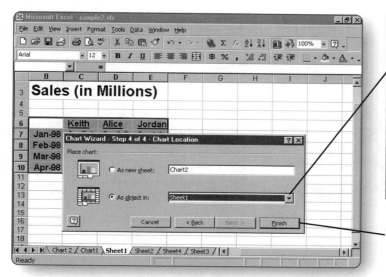

NOTE

By default, the sheet from which the data is taken appears in the As object in: box. You can open this drop-down list and choose a different existing sheet in the workbook for the chart position if you want.

16. Click on **Finish**.

The chart will appear either in the current worksheet or in a new worksheet called Chart1, depending on your selection in step 15.

The Chart toolbar will also open.

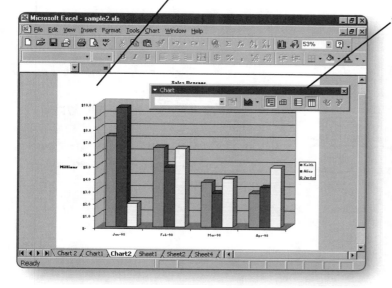

Changing the Chart Type

You can change to a different chart type at any time, without re-creating the chart.

1. Click on the **chart** you want to work with. The chart will be selected.

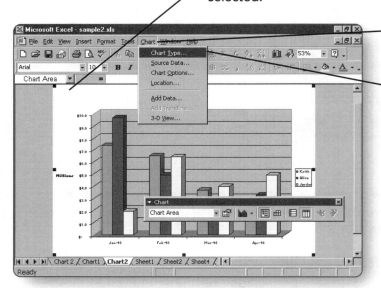

2. Click on **Chart**. The Chart menu will appear.

3. Click on **Chart Type**. The Chart Type dialog box will open.

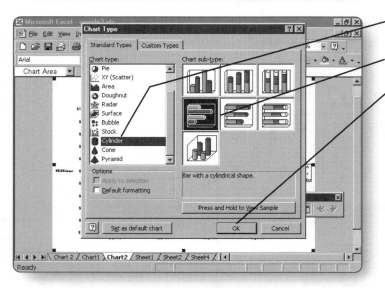

4. Click on a new **chart type**.

5. Click on a new **sub-type**.

6. Click on **OK**. The chart type will change for the selected chart.

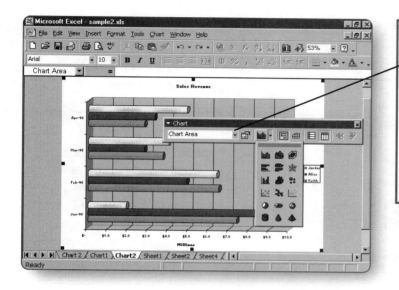

TIP

Another way to change chart types is to click the down arrow (▼) next to the Chart Type button on the Chart toolbar. A list of common chart types pops up; click on the one you want.

Changing How the Data Is Plotted

In the example charts you have seen so far in this chapter, the horizontal axis shows months, and each different color bar represents a person. This invites the reader to compare the performance of the salespeople against one another.

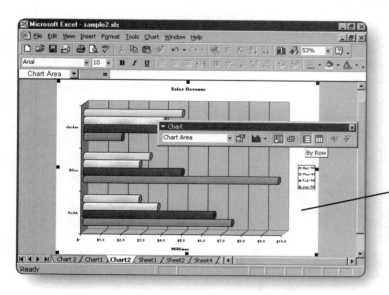

Alternatively, you could plot the same data so that people's names appear on the horizontal axis, and each bar color represents a month. This would invite the reader to compare each person's performance month-by-month individually.

1. Click on the **chart** you want to work with. The chart will be selected.

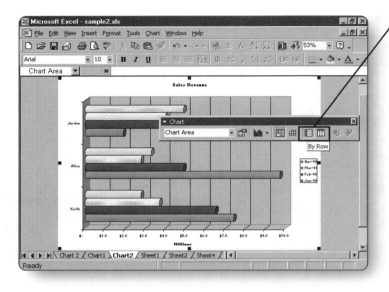

2. Click on the **By Column** or **By Row button** on the Chart toolbar. The way the data is plotted will change.

NOTE

If the Chart toolbar does not appear and you need to use it, choose View, Toolbars, Chart from the Excel menu.

Changing Which Cells Are Plotted

You can also change the range of cells on which the chart is based.

1. Click on the **chart** you want to work with. The chart will be selected.

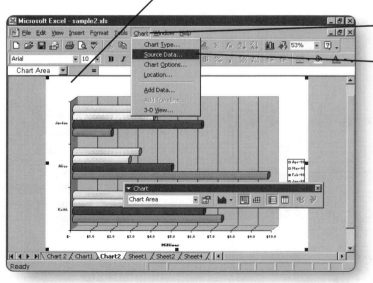

2. Click on **Chart**.

3. Click on **Source Data**. The Source Data dialog box will open.

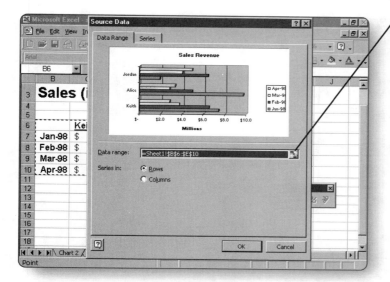

4. Click on the **Collapse Dialog button.** The dialog box will shrink to a title bar and a single line.

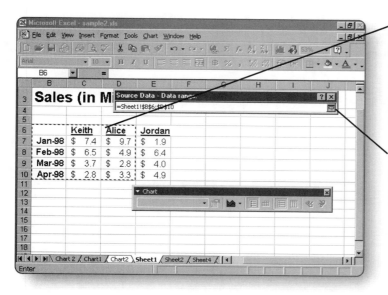

5. Drag across the **cells** you want to use. You might, for example, exclude a certain month or salesperson that you previously included. The cells will be highlighted.

6. Click on the **Expand Dialog button.** The dialog box will reappear.

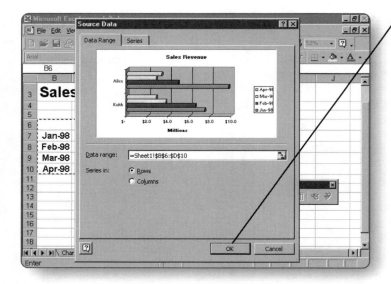

7. **Click** on **OK**. The chart will show the new range.

16

Formatting Your Chart

Excel has many formatting capabilities that can make your chart look even better. In this chapter, you'll learn how to:

- Improve label readability
- Add series labels
- Add a legend
- Format individual parts of a chart

Making Labels Easier to Read

Although the wizard formats the chart, you may need to make some changes to improve its readability.

Changing Label Size and Color

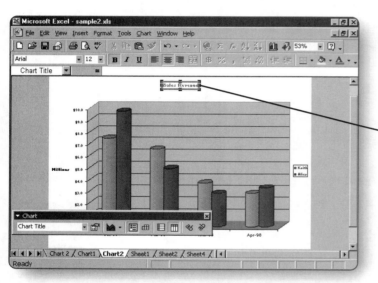

Labels on a chart are often too small at their default size. You may want to make them larger and dress them up with some color.

1. Click on the **title**. A box with selection handles will appear around it.

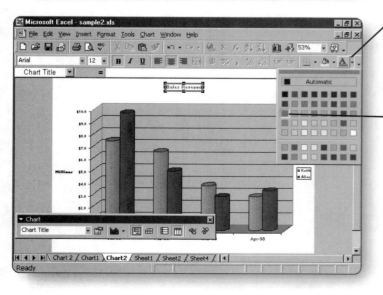

2. Click on the **down arrow** (▼) next to the Font Color button. The color palette will open.

3. Click on a **color** that will be more visible against the background color in your chart. The new color will appear on the title.

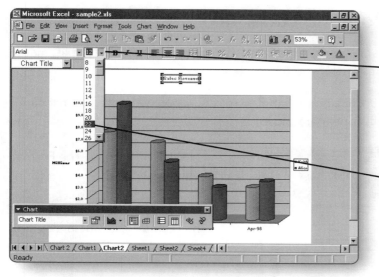

If the text is still a little small, you can change the font size.

4. Click on the **down arrow** (▼) next to the Font Size button, while the title is still selected. A drop-down list will appear.

5. Click on a **larger size**. The title will appear in the new size.

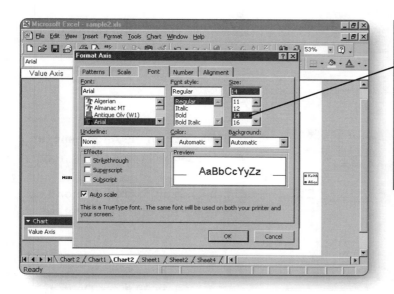

TIP

To change the font or font size for the axis labels, double-click on the axis to open the Format Axis dialog box. On the Font tab, choose a larger font size, and then click OK.

Rotating Label Text

Some labels, especially labels along the vertical (Y) axis, may look better rotated 90 degrees.

1. Click on the **label** to rotate. A box with selection handles will appear around it.

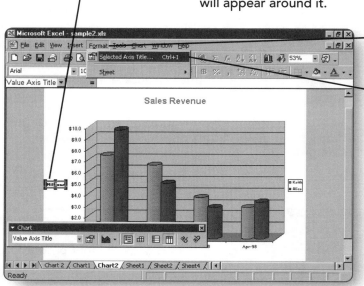

2. Click on Format. The Format menu will appear.

3. Click on **Selected Axis Title**. The Format Axis Title dialog box will open.

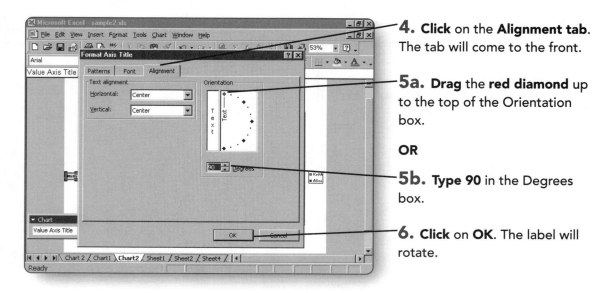

4. Click on the **Alignment tab**. The tab will come to the front.

5a. Drag the **red diamond** up to the top of the Orientation box.

OR

5b. Type 90 in the Degrees box.

6. Click on **OK**. The label will rotate.

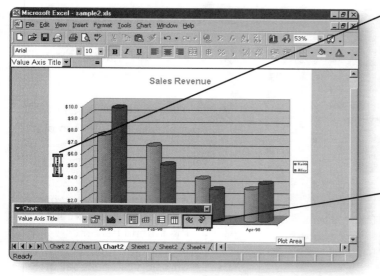

When you place a vertical axis label parallel to a chart, there is more room for the chart, and the chart expands to fill the available space. Adjusting label rotation and positioning is one way to make a chart appear bigger without allocating more space on a worksheet for it.

If you want to rotate a particular label by 45 degrees up or down, you can use the Angle Text Downward and Angle Text Upward buttons on the Chart toolbar.

Adding Data Labels

On most bar and column charts, it's easy to find the value of a particular bar. Just follow its top to the value axis and read the number there. However, in some chart types, such as pie and scatter, it is not so easy to identify a value. In such cases, data labels can help.

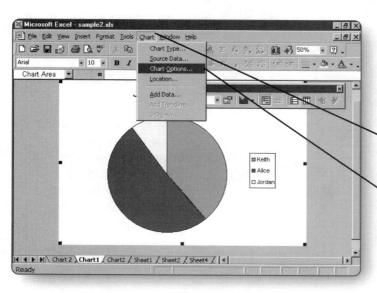

1. **Click** on the a **chart**. The chart will be selected.

2. **Click** on **Chart**. The Chart menu will appear.

3. **Click** on **Chart Options**. The Chart Options dialog box will open.

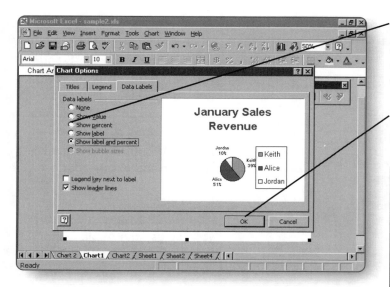

4. **Click** on a **data label type**. Show percent is good for pie charts; Show value works well for many other types.

5. **Click** on **OK**. The chart will appear with the labels in place.

TIP

If you use Show label or Show label and percent, the legend becomes redundant. You can turn it off using the next set of steps.

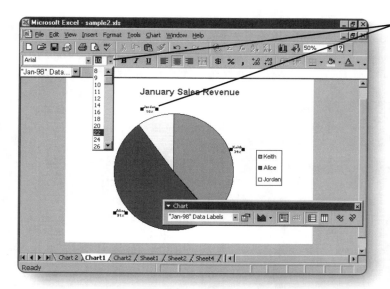

If the data labels are too small, as they are here, you can easily resize them. Just click on one of them (which selects them all), and then choose a different font size from the Font Size drop-down list.

TIP

The labels appear outside the pie slices by default, but you can move them on top of the slices if you prefer. See the following section to learn how to move labels.

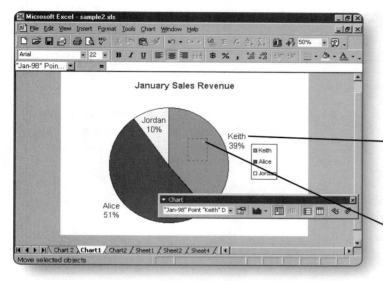

Moving Labels

Labels each appear in their own floating box, and you can drag those boxes anywhere on the chart.

1. Click on the **label** you want to move. A box with selection handles will appear around the label.

2. Click on the **border** of the label box and **drag** it to a new location. The box will be moved.

Resizing the Legend

The *legend* is the key that tells what each color or pattern represents. By default it may be very small; follow these steps to make it larger.

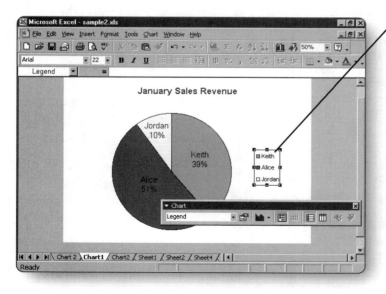

1. Click on the **legend**. Click on the outer box of the legend rather than on an individual label within it. The legend will be selected.

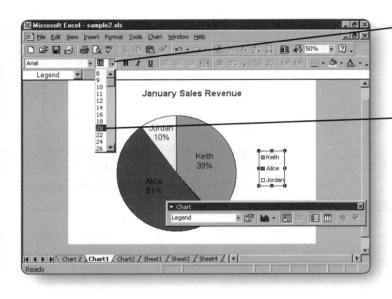

2. Click on the **down arrow** (▼) next to the Font Size control on the toolbar. The Font Size drop-down list will open.

3. Click on a **larger number**, such as 20. The size of the text in the legend will increase.

Displaying or Hiding the Legend

If you add data labels to a chart, the legend may become unnecessary. If so, you can hide it. Do not hide the legend, however, if it is needed to help the reader understand the chart.

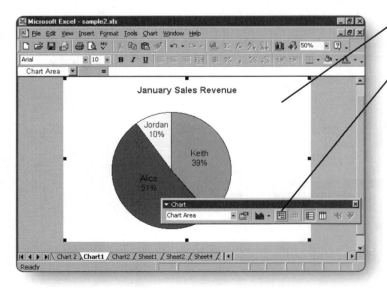

1. Click on the **chart** to select it. The Chart toolbar will appear.

2. Click on the **Legend button** on the Chart toolbar to toggle between showing and hiding the legend.

Displaying or Hiding a Data Table

If the chart is on the same sheet as your data, a data table is redundant. However, if the chart is on a separate sheet, a data table can help the reader by providing the data on which the chart was based.

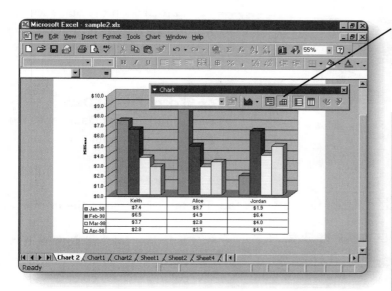

1. Click on the **Data Table button** on the Chart toolbar to toggle between displaying and hiding the data table.

NOTE

If you use a data table, you do not need a legend because the legend is built in. You can make the text in the data table bigger the same way that you did with the legend in the previous section.

Formatting Chart Elements

Each element of a chart has its own formatting settings. For example, the chart walls, chart floor, legend, each different colored bar or slice, each label, and each axis can be formatted separately. Just right-click on any element and choose its Format command from the shortcut menu. The exact name of the command depends on the chosen element.

The following sections show a few examples of this flexible procedure.

Changing Series Colors

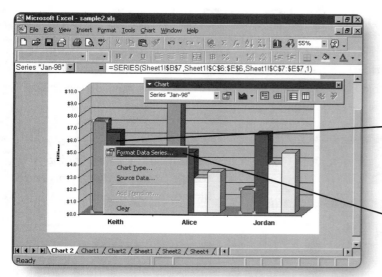

One series is distinguished from another by color. You can change the colors used in the chart to any colors you like (for example, your company's official colors).

1. Right-click on the **bar**, **slice**, or **other series shape** that you want to change. A shortcut menu will appear.

2. Click on **Format Data Series**. The Format Data Series dialog box will open.

3. Click on the **Patterns tab**. The tab will come to the front.

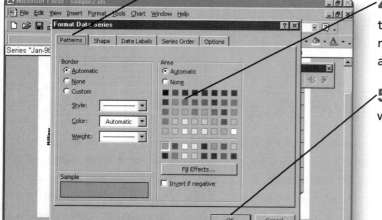

4. Click on a **colored square** in the Area section to choose a new color. The new color will appear in the Sample area.

5. Click on **OK**. The new color will appear in the chart.

TIP

You can click the Fill Effects button in the Format Data Series dialog box to choose special effects such as textures, patterns, and gradients. This is available in the Format dialog box not only for data series but also for walls, backgrounds, and any other chart elements.

Setting a Number Format for an Axis

If the numbers on your value axis (usually the vertical axis) represent a certain unit, such as dollars, you may want to format them as such.

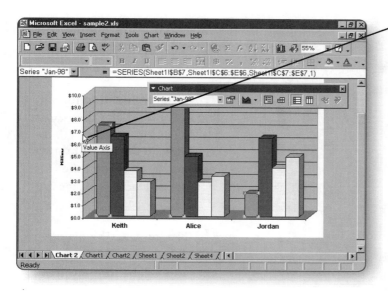

1. Point the **mouse** at the **axis** that contains the values. A ScreenTip will appear saying "Value Axis." If it says anything different, you are pointing at the wrong spot; reposition the pointer.

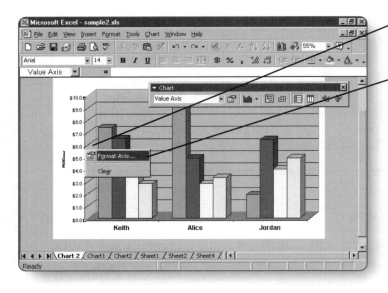

2. Right-click. A shortcut menu will appear.

3. Click on **Format Axis**. The Format Axis dialog box will open.

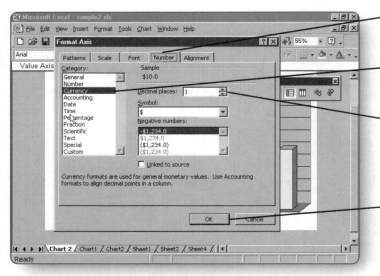

4. Click on the **Number tab**. The tab will come to the front.

5. Click on a number format **category**, such as Currency.

6. Click on the **up and down arrows (◆)** to change the number of Decimal places if desired.

7. Click on **OK**. The dialog box will close and the numbers on that axis will be formatted as you specified.

17

Creating a Map

Business data is often related to geographic areas. Excel has a great feature that enables you to plot data directly on a map. In this chapter, you'll learn how to:

- Create a map
- Add labels and text to the map
- Add features such as cities, airports, or highways
- Place the map in your worksheet

Making a Map

In this example, the worksheet contains Australian sales data by state. You can create a map to display this data.

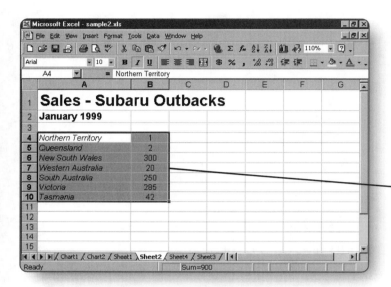

1. Click and **drag** the **mouse arrow** across the columns with the state names and sales data. The cells will be highlighted.

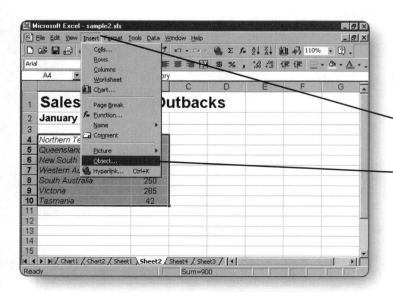

2. Click on **Insert**. The Insert menu will appear.

3. Click on **Object**. The Object dialog box will open.

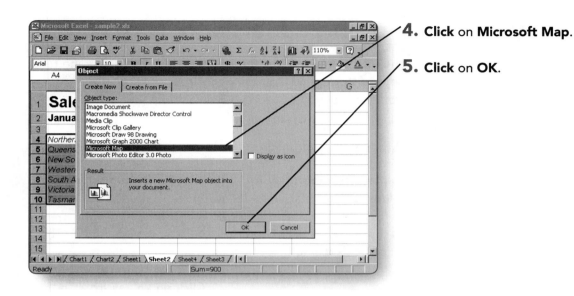

4. **Click** on **Microsoft Map**.

5. **Click** on **OK**.

The Map toolbar will replace the standard toolbars.

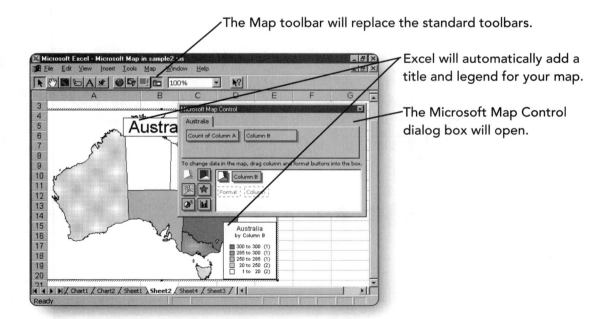

Excel will automatically add a title and legend for your map.

The Microsoft Map Control dialog box will open.

Adding Labels and Text

The effectiveness of the map can be improved by adding text beyond the legend. You can either add labels from the worksheet or you can add your own text.

Adding Labels

You can add labels that show either the state names or the values for each state. The following steps add the values.

1. **Click** on the **Map Labels button** on the Map toolbar. The Map Labels dialog box will open.

2. **Click** on **Values from:** in the Create labels from box. The item will be highlighted. If you wanted to add the state names, you would choose Map feature names here instead.

3. **Click** on **OK**. The Map Labels dialog box will close.

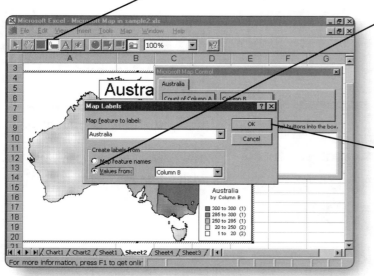

4. Move the **mouse arrow** across the map. Notice that the correct sales number will appear as you move the mouse arrow across the corresponding state.

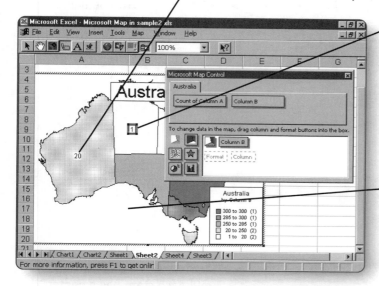

5. Click in the **appropriate state** to place the sales number on the map. Selection handles will appear around the number.

6. Repeat steps 4 and **5** to add the remaining sales numbers for each state.

7. Click anywhere on the background of the map. The label-adding mode will be cancelled, and the mouse pointer will turn into an arrow again.

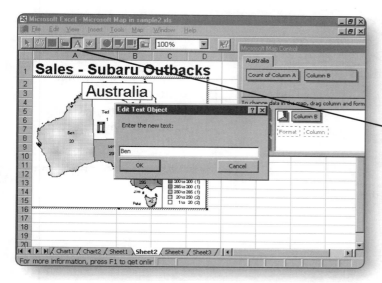

Adding Text

You can add text to the map. In this example, the names of the salesmen will be added.

1. Click on the **Add Text button** on the Map toolbar. The mouse arrow will change to an I-beam when you move it back over the worksheet area.

2. Click on **the spot** where you want to add text. The Edit Text Object dialog box will appear.

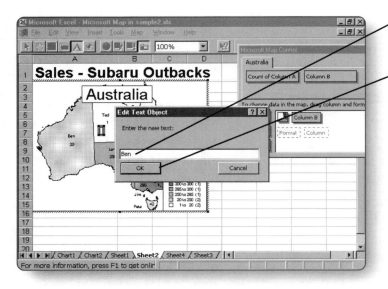

3. Type a **name** in the dialog box.

4. Click on **OK**. The name will appear on the map.

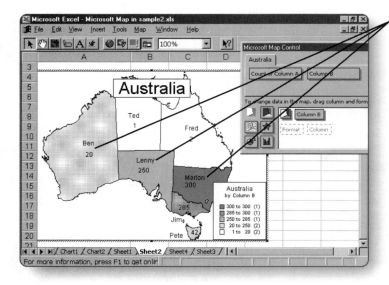

5. Repeat steps 2 through **4** until each state has a name added.

NOTE

You can drag the names around on the map to reposition them just as you do with any object in Excel.

Adding Cities, Highways, and Airports

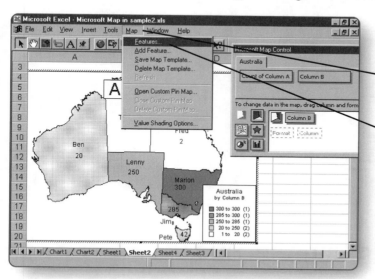

Excel has more built-in features that you can add to your map.

1. Click on **Map**. The Map menu will appear.

2. Click on **Features**. The Map Features dialog box will open.

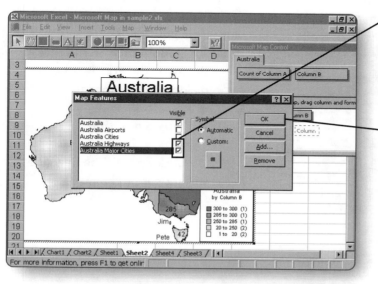

3. Click on **Australia Highways** and **Australia Major Cities** to use those features in your map. A ✔ will appear in the boxes next to those items.

4. Click on **OK**. The Map Features dialog box will close.

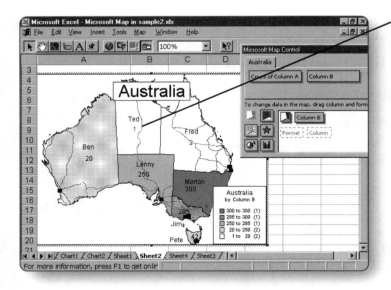

Now you can see why Ben only sold one vehicle. There aren't a lot of roads in the Northern Territory!

Editing the Title

The default title for a map is the geographical area name. If the audience will recognize the region without a title, you may want to edit the title of the map to say something more meaningful.

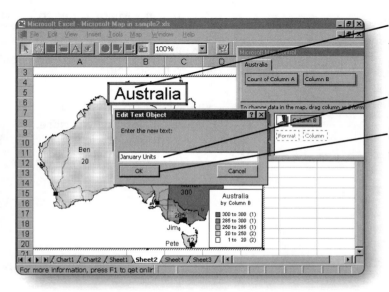

1. Double-click on the **title** in the map. The Edit Text Object dialog box will appear.

2. Type a new **title**.

3. Click on **OK**. The new title will appear on the map.

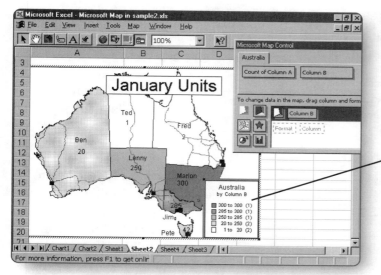

Editing the Legend

You can also edit the legend, to make its title more meaningful for the map.

1. Double-click on the **legend**. The Format Properties dialog box will open.

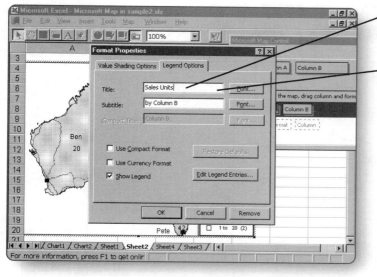

2. Click in the **Title: text box**. The text will be highlighted.

3a. Type to **add a new title** to the legend.

OR

3b. Press the **Delete key** to eliminate the title.

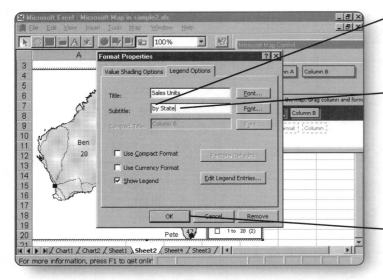

4. **Click** in the **Subtitle: text box**. The text will be highlighted.

5a. **Type** to **add a new subtitle** to the legend.

OR

5b. **Press** the **Delete key** to eliminate the subtitle.

6. **Click** on **OK**. The Format Properties dialog box will close.

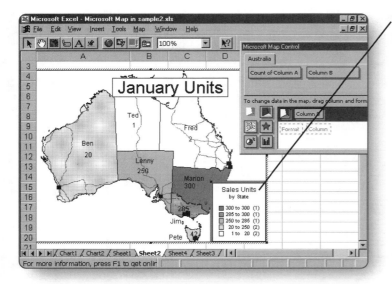

The changes you made to the legend will appear in the map.

Placing the Map in the Worksheet

While you're working on the map, it's an independent object that hasn't been embedded in the worksheet yet. When you've added all the text and features you need, you're ready to add it to the worksheet.

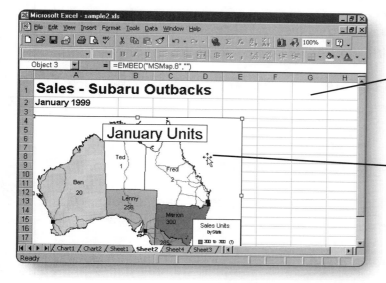

1. Click in the **worksheet**. The Map toolbar will disappear, and the map will become part of the worksheet.

2. Move the **mouse arrow** across the map. The mouse arrow will change to a four-headed arrow.

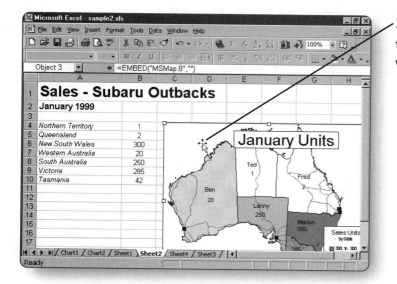

3. Click on the **map** and **drag** it to where you want it to appear within your worksheet.

Part IV Review Questions

1. How do you access the Excel Chart Wizard? *See "Creating a Chart with the Chart Wizard" in Chapter 15*

2. What type of chart is limited to a single series of data? *See "Creating a Chart with the Chart Wizard" in Chapter 15*

3. How do you change a chart's type without re-creating it entirely? *See "Changing the Chart Type" in Chapter 15*

4. How do you switch between charting by rows and charting by columns? *See "Changing How the Data Is Plotted" in Chapter 15*

5. How do you make the chart refer to other cells? *See "Changing Which Cells Are Plotted" in Chapter 15*

6. When might you want to use data labels to indicate the values on a chart? *See "Adding Data Labels" in Chapter 16*

7. What is a legend? *See "Resizing the Legend" in Chapter 16*

8. To format a part of the chart, you right-click on it and then select what command? *See "Formatting Chart Elements" in Chapter 16*

9. What is the Excel map feature useful for? *See the introduction in Chapter 17*

10. What must you do to ensure that Excel recognizes that it's working with geographical data? *See "Making a Map" in Chapter 17*

PART V

Putting Excel to Work

18

Exploring Functions Further

Excel includes more than 300 functions, some of which you may never use. However, many of the functions can make your daily work with Excel much easier. In this chapter, you'll learn how to:

- Work with statistical functions
- Work with financial functions

Working with Statistical Functions

Statistical functions such as MAXIMUM, MINIMUM, and AVERAGE are popular in worksheets because they can do much of the number crunching for you. For example, you can figure out the average of a column of numbers by using the AVERAGE function, or you can total a column of numbers by using the SUM function.

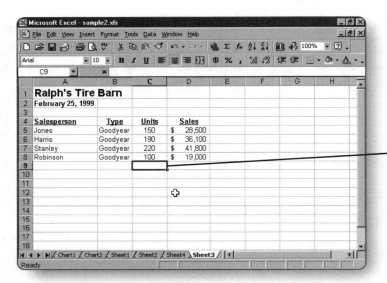

1. Click in the **cell** where you want to calculate the average of a column. The cell will become active.

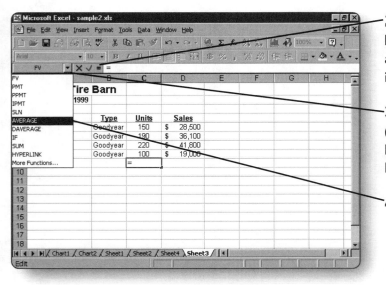

2. Click on the **Edit Formula button**. The equal sign will appear in the Formula bar and in the cell you selected.

3. Click on the **down arrow** (▼) to the right of the Function box. The Function drop-down list will appear.

4. Click on **AVERAGE**.

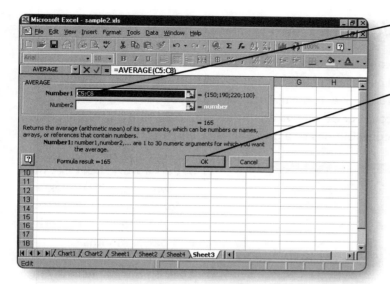

The function dialog box will open—with Excel's best guess entered in the Number1 field.

5. Click on **OK**. The dialog box will close, and the average will appear in the cell.

In this example, the average of cells C5 through C8 (165) appears in C9.

Working with Financial Functions

Excel has some powerful functions that can make working with financial data much easier. One of those functions is *FV* or Future Value. It calculates how much you will have in a savings account or other investment account based on a certain number of contributions of a given amount and a certain interest rate.

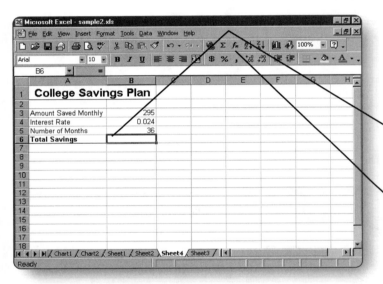

1. Set up a **worksheet** like the one shown here, with values and labels for the amount you plan to save, the interest rate, and the number of months.

2. Click on the **cell** where you want to enter the function. The cell will become active.

3. Click on the **Paste Function button**. The Paste Function dialog box will open.

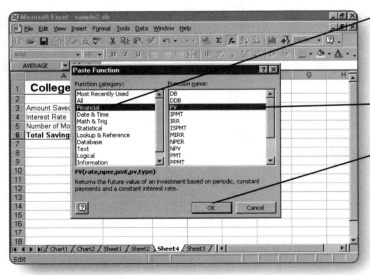

4. Click on **Financial** on the Function category: list. A list of functions in that category will appear.

5. Click on **FV** on the Function name: list.

6. Click on **OK**. The Formula palette will appear, showing the needed arguments.

7. Drag the **Formula palette** to the side so that the cells you are working with are visible.

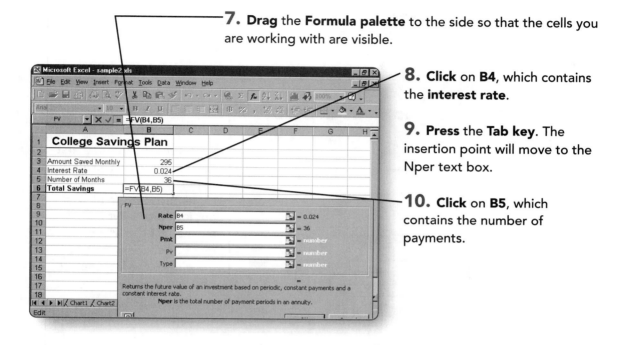

8. Click on **B4**, which contains the **interest rate**.

9. Press the **Tab key**. The insertion point will move to the Nper text box.

10. Click on **B5**, which contains the number of payments.

11. Press the **Tab key**. The insertion point will move to the Pmt text box.

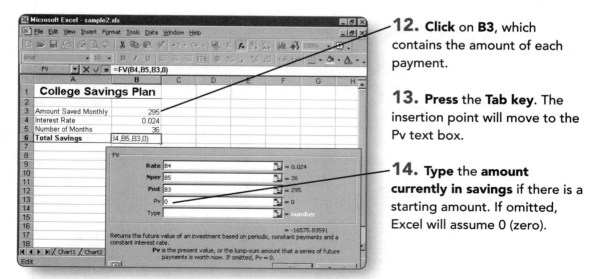

12. Click on **B3**, which contains the amount of each payment.

13. Press the **Tab key**. The insertion point will move to the Pv text box.

14. Type the **amount currently in savings** if there is a starting amount. If omitted, Excel will assume 0 (zero).

15. Press the **Tab key**. The insertion point will move to the Type text box.

16. Type 1 in the Type box.

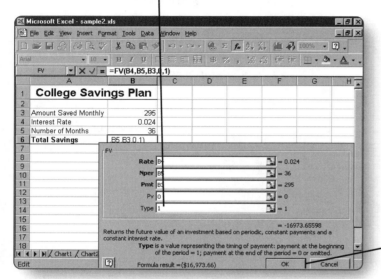

NOTE

Type 1 means that the first payment (the first savings deposit) is made on the same day that the plan is put into place. Type 0 means that the first payment or deposit is made at the end of the first period (the first month).

17. Click on **OK**. The total amount saved will appear in the cell.

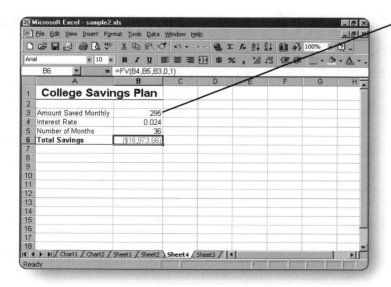

You can play "what if" by changing the numbers in one or more of the cells on which the calculation is based. For example, you might increase the interest rate to see how your savings would grow faster.

19

Creating Depreciation Tables

You can use Excel to calculate the *depreciation*, the reduction in value, of an asset. In this chapter, you'll learn how to:

- Set up a depreciation table
- Calculate a straight line depreciation amount
- Calculate a decreasing book value

Making a Depreciation Table

A depreciation table determines how much the value of an asset decreases over a set amount a time. You can begin creating the table by typing the labels of the rows.

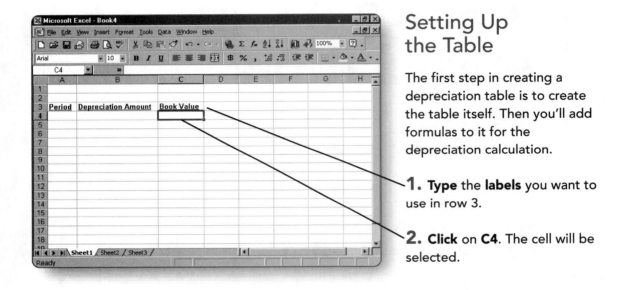

Setting Up the Table

The first step in creating a depreciation table is to create the table itself. Then you'll add formulas to it for the depreciation calculation.

1. Type the **labels** you want to use in row 3.

2. Click on **C4**. The cell will be selected.

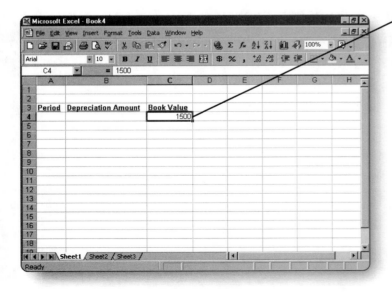

3. Type the **original cost** and press **Enter**. The amount will appear in the cell.

Entering the Depreciation Periods

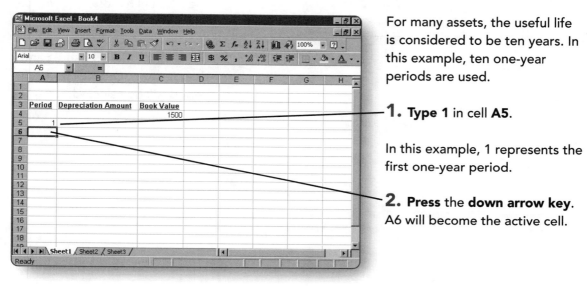

For many assets, the useful life is considered to be ten years. In this example, ten one-year periods are used.

1. Type 1 in cell **A5**.

In this example, 1 represents the first one-year period.

2. Press the **down arrow key**. A6 will become the active cell.

3. Click on the **Edit Formula button**. The Formula palette will appear.

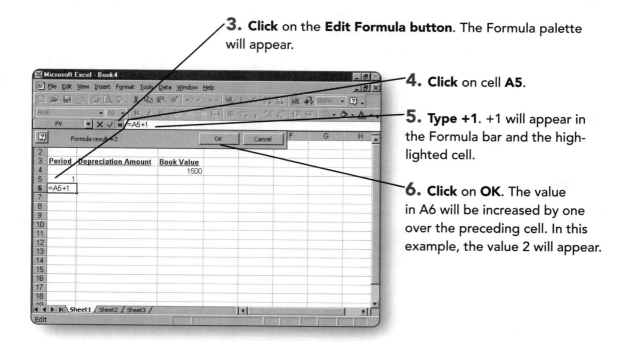

4. Click on cell **A5**.

5. Type +1. +1 will appear in the Formula bar and the highlighted cell.

6. Click on **OK**. The value in A6 will be increased by one over the preceding cell. In this example, the value 2 will appear.

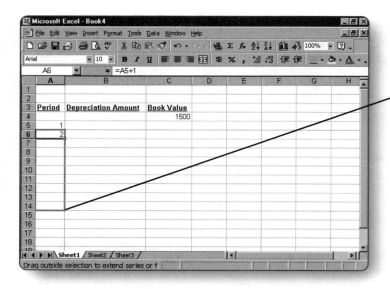

7. Move the **mouse arrow** over the **Fill handle**. The mouse arrow will change to a plus sign.

8. Click on the **Fill handle** and **drag** it down. One cell for each period will be selected.

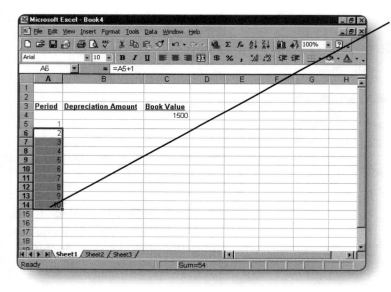

9. Release the **mouse button**. Excel will fill the cells with increasing values.

Calculating the
Straight Line Depreciation

Straight line depreciation means that the depreciation of an asset is divided equally throughout the periods.

1. **Click** on **B5**. The cell will become active.

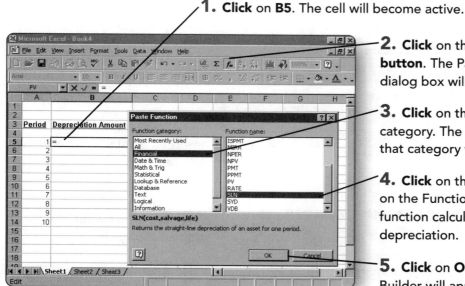

2. **Click** on the **Paste Function button**. The Paste Function dialog box will open.

3. **Click** on the **Financial** category. The list of functions in that category will appear.

4. **Click** on the **SLN function** on the Function name: list. This function calculates straight line depreciation.

5. **Click** on **OK**. The Function Builder will appear.

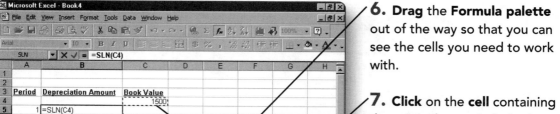

6. **Drag** the **Formula palette** out of the way so that you can see the cells you need to work with.

7. **Click** on the **cell** containing the original cost. A dashed marquee will appear around the cell, and the cell address will appear in the Cost text box.

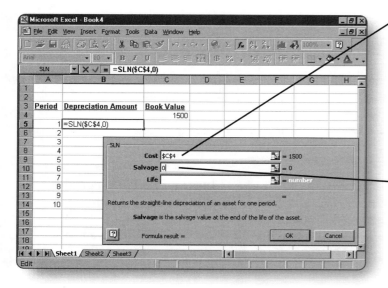

8. Press the **F4 key**. Dollar signs will appear in the cell reference, indicating that this is an absolute reference.

9. Press the **Tab key**. The insertion point will move to the Salvage text box.

10. Type the **value** of the asset at the end of the ten-year period.

11. Press the **Tab key**. The insertion point will move to the Life text box.

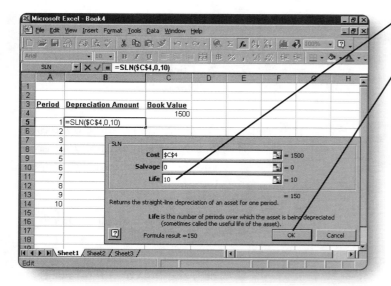

12. Type the **number** of depreciation periods.

13. Click on **OK**. The Straight Line depreciation amount to be used for each period will appear in B5.

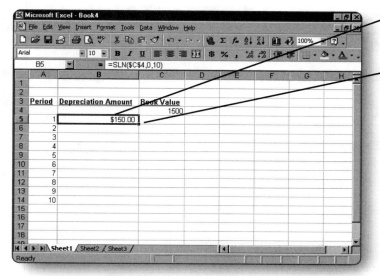

In this example, $150 is the depreciation amount.

14. Move the **mouse pointer** over the **Fill handle**. The pointer will change to a plus sign.

> **NOTE**
> Excel automatically formats the straight line depreciation amount as currency.

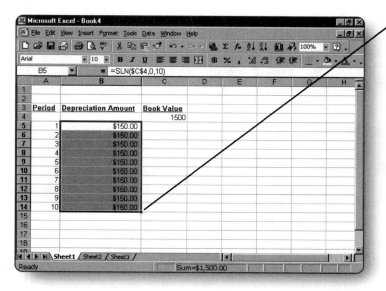

15. Click on the **Fill handle** and **drag** it down. One cell for each depreciation period will be selected.

16. Release the **mouse button**. Excel will fill each of the cells with the same straight line depreciation amount.

Calculating the Book Value for Each Depreciation Period

Now you are ready to calculate the changing depreciation.

1. **Click** on **C5**. The cell will become active.

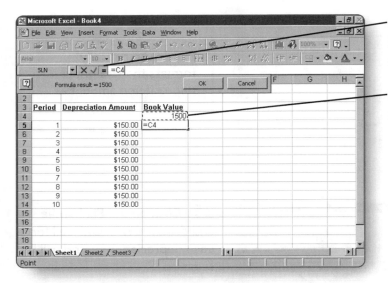

2. **Click** on the **Edit Formula button**. The Formula palette will appear.

3. **Click** on **C4** (the original cost).

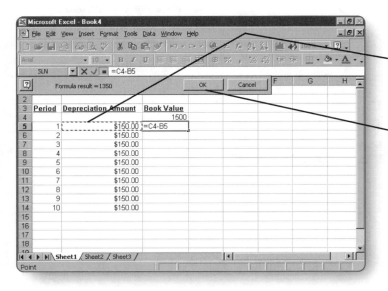

4. **Type** –.

5. **Click** on **B5** (the depreciation amount for the first period).

6. **Click** on **OK**. The original cost will decrease by the depreciation amount for the first period.

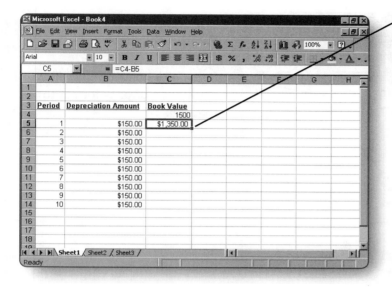

7. **Move** the **mouse arrow** over the **Fill handle**. The mouse arrow will change to a plus sign.

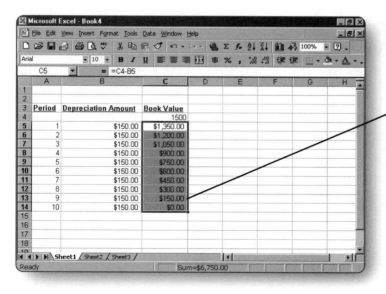

8. **Click** on the **Fill handle** and **drag** it down. One cell for each depreciation period will be selected.

9. **Release** the **mouse button**. Excel will fill each of the cells with the decreasing book value.

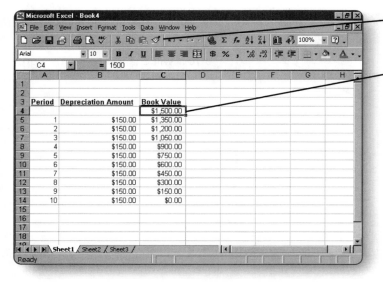

10. **Click** on the **Format Paintbrush button**.

11. **Click** on **C4**. Excel will apply the Currency format to that cell.

20

Setting Up Amortization Tables

If you have a loan of $2,000 and you have to pay it off in ten months, an amortization table can give you some important information. You can use Excel to calculate the interest, principal, and total payment involved in the repayment of the loan. In this chapter, you'll learn how to:

- Set up labels for an amortization table
- Compute the interest amount of a payment
- Determine the principal amount of a payment
- Figure out the amount of a payment
- Calculate the decreasing balance

Creating an Amortization Table

Your table needs four columns for making calculations. You need to calculate how much each payment is, how much of the payment is interest, how much of the payment is principal (and actually reduces the balance), and what the balance is after you make each payment. You also need a fifth column for assigning a number to each payment.

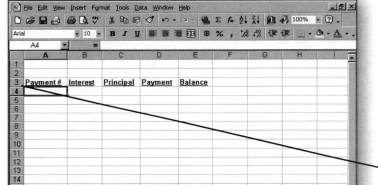

Typing the Labels for a Table

You can begin your amortization table by preparing labels for the columns.

1. **Type** the **labels** you want to use in row 3.

Setting Up the Column for the Payment Numbers

The first column, Payment Number, assigns a number to each payment.

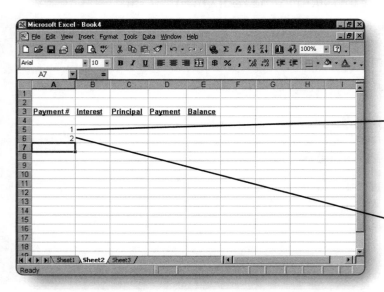

1. **Type** 1 in **A5**.

2. **Press** the **Enter key**. The next cell in the column will be selected.

3. **Type** 2 in **A6**.

4. **Press** the **Enter key**. The next cell in the column will be selected.

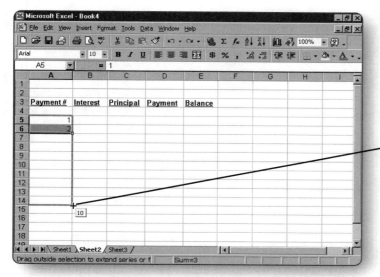

5. Click on **A5** and **drag** to **A6**. Both cells will be selected.

6. Move the **mouse arrow** over the **Fill handle**. The mouse arrow will become a plus sign.

7. Click on the **Fill handle** and **drag** it down until you see a small box containing the number of payments you will be making.

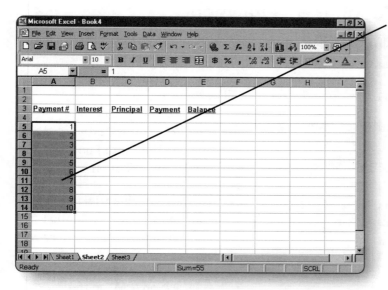

8. Release the **mouse button**. The payment numbers will appear in the cells.

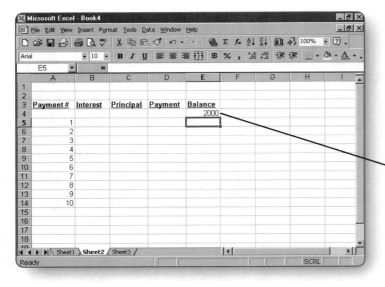

Entering the Balance

Before you can calculate the interest per payment, you must place the beginning balance in the Balance column.

1. Type the loan amount (for example, 2000) in cell **E4** (the first cell in the Balance column).

2. Press the **Enter key**.

Calculating the Interest Amount of a Payment

Now you are ready to calculate the amount of your payment eaten up by interest.

1. Click on **B5**. The cell will become active.

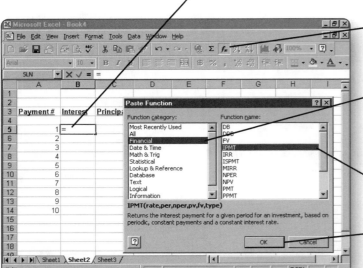

2. Click on the **Paste Function button**. The Paste Function dialog box will open.

3. Click on **Financial** in the Function category: list. The list of functions in that category will appear.

4. Click on **IPMT** in the Function name: list.

5. Click on **OK**. The Formula palette will open showing the function's arguments.

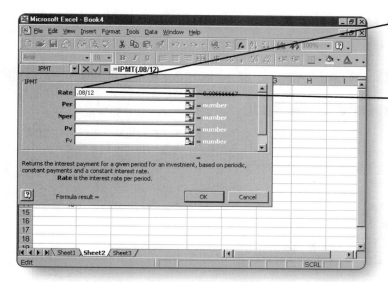

6. **Type** the **annual interest rate** as a decimal (for example, .08 for 8%).

7. **Type /12**. This divides the annual interest rate by 12 to arrive at a monthly rate.

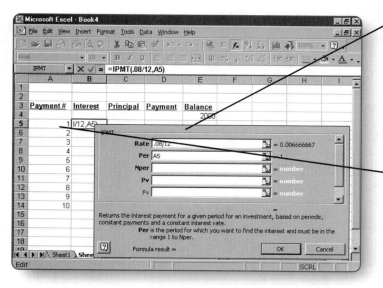

8. **Drag** the **Formula palette** to the side so that you can see the cells you are working with.

9. **Press** the **Tab key**. The insertion point will move to the Per text box.

10. **Click** on **A5**, which contains the first payment number.

11. Press the **Tab key**. The insertion point will move to the Nper text box.

12. Type the **number of periods** (for example, 10).

13. Press the **Tab key**. The insertion point will move to the Pv text box.

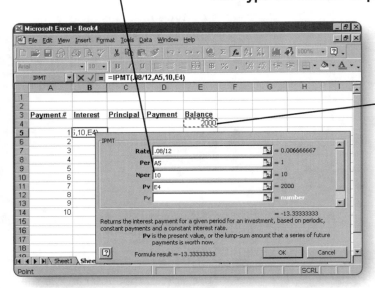

14. Click on **E4**, which contains the beginning balance.

15. Press the **Tab key**. The insertion point will move to the Fv text box.

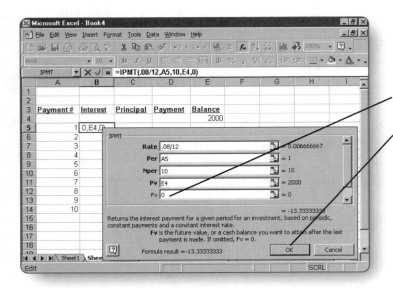

16. Type the **ending balance**.

17. Click on **OK**.

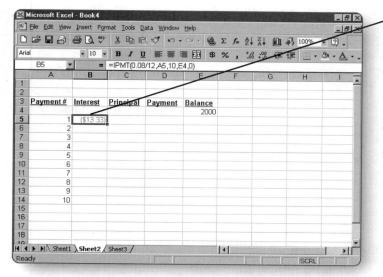

The interest amount, $13.33 in this example, will appear in the cell.

Calculating the Principal Amount of a Payment

The next calculation is the principal amount of the payment—the amount that the payment makes your balance drop.

1. **Click** on **C5** (the first payment's row in the Principal column). The cell will become active.

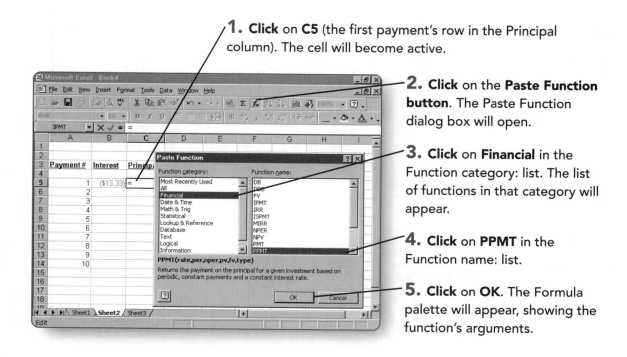

2. **Click** on the **Paste Function button**. The Paste Function dialog box will open.

3. **Click** on **Financial** in the Function category: list. The list of functions in that category will appear.

4. **Click** on **PPMT** in the Function name: list.

5. **Click** on **OK**. The Formula palette will appear, showing the function's arguments.

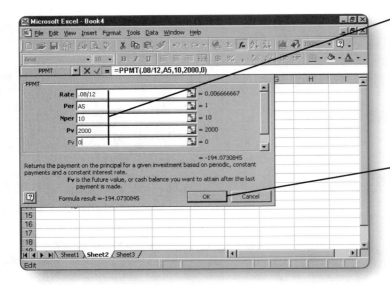

6. Enter the **appropriate values** in the PPMT function dialog box. Use the same values that you used in the IPMT function in the preceding steps, or simply copy the values from this illustration.

7. Click on **OK**. The PPMT function dialog box will close.

The principal amount of the payment, $194.07 in this example, will appear.

Entering the Payment Amount

Next, you enter the payment amount in the Payment column.

1. Click on **D5**, which is the first payment row's cell in the Payment column. The cell will become active.

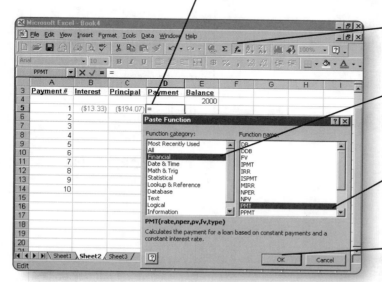

2. Click on the **Paste Function button**. The Paste Function dialog box will open.

3. Click on **Financial** in the Function category: list. A list of the functions in that category will appear.

4. Click on **PMT** in the Function name: list. The item will be highlighted.

5. Click on **OK**. The Formula palette appears showing the arguments for the function.

6. Enter the **appropriate values** in the PMT function dialog box. Use the same values that you used in the last two sets of steps, or copy the values from this illustration.

NOTE

There is a small difference between the values here and in earlier steps; the Per box is not present.

7. **Type 1** or **0** in the Type text box.

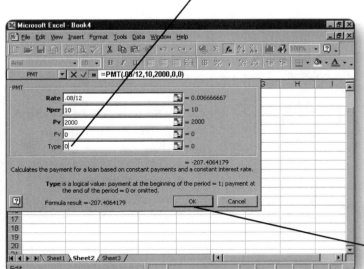

8. **Click** on **OK**. The PMT dialog box will close.

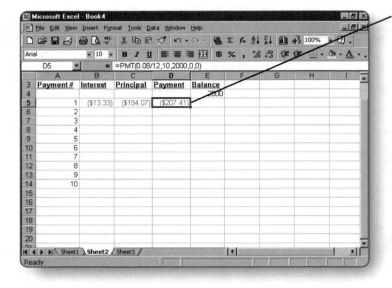

The payment amount, $207.41 in this example, will appear.

Calculating the Decreasing Balance

In the Balance column, you begin to see the results of all that outgoing money.

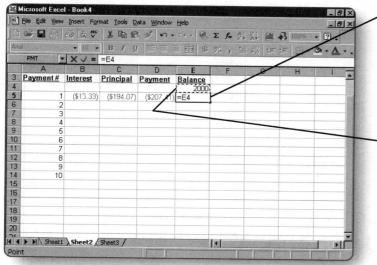

1. Click on **E5**, the first empty cell under the heading in the Balance column. The cell will become active.

2. Type =.

3. Click on **E4**, the cell containing the beginning balance. A marquee will appear around the cell.

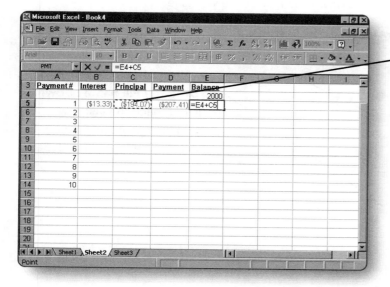

4. Type +.

5. Click on **C5**, the cell containing the principal. A marquee will appear around the cell.

6. Press Enter. The formula will be entered in E5.

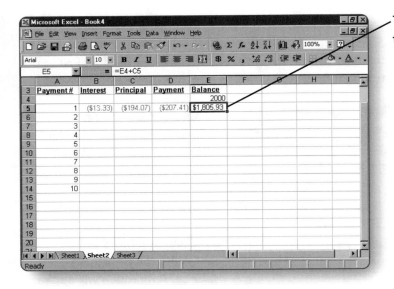

The new balance, $1,805.93 in this example, will appear.

Copying the Formulas Down the Worksheet

Now that you've taken the time to enter the formulas in the first calculated row of the worksheet, you can just copy the formulas down the rest of the worksheet.

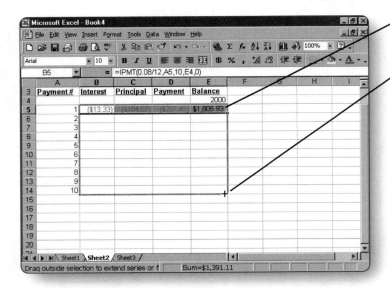

1. **Click** on **B5** and **drag** to **E5**. The range will be highlighted.

2. **Drag** the **Fill handle down** until you reach the last row containing a payment number in column A. The formulas will be copied.

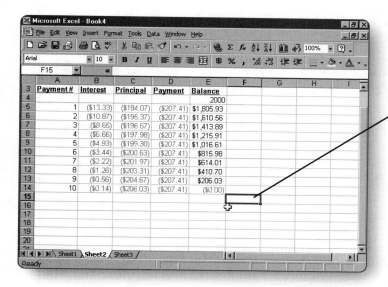

3. Release the **mouse button**. Excel will fill the cells with the data resulting from the copied formulas.

4. Click outside the selected range. Excel will remove the highlighting so that you can see the completed amortization table.

21

Integrating Excel with Word

Excel and Word work together smoothly so that you easily can combine an Excel worksheet with a Word document. For example, you can have a memo created in Word that contains an Excel worksheet. In this chapter, you'll learn how to:

- Create an Excel worksheet from within Word
- Format a new Excel worksheet
- Insert rows or columns in a new Excel worksheet
- Insert an existing Excel worksheet into a Word document

Creating an Excel Worksheet from Within Word

One way to get an Excel worksheet into a Word document is to cut and paste it. That method involves first creating the worksheet in Excel, copying it, and then pasting it into a Word document. But you can create an Excel worksheet in a Word document without having to create the worksheet in Excel first.

You can create an Excel worksheet right in a Word document by using the Insert Microsoft Excel Worksheet button. The worksheet you create is actually part of the Word document, and when you save the Word file, this spreadsheet is saved as part of the document. This is called *embedding* a worksheet in Word.

1. **Type text** in the Word document.

2. **Click** in the **Word document** where you want your Excel worksheet to appear. The insertion point will be placed.

3. **Click** on the **Insert Microsoft Excel Worksheet button**. A grid of boxes will appear beneath the button.

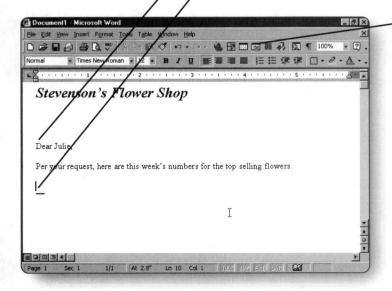

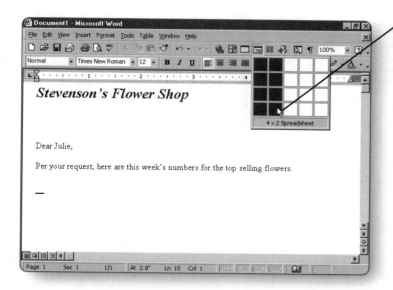

4. **Move** the **mouse arrow** over the palette until you see the number of columns and rows you want at the bottom of the palette.

5. **Click** to select the number of rows and columns.

An Excel screen containing a worksheet, menu bar, and toolbar will appear within the Word document, but the Microsoft Word title bar will remain.

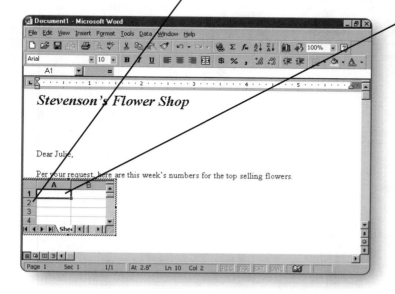

6. **Click** in the **cell** where you want to enter data. Excel will highlight the cell with a dark border.

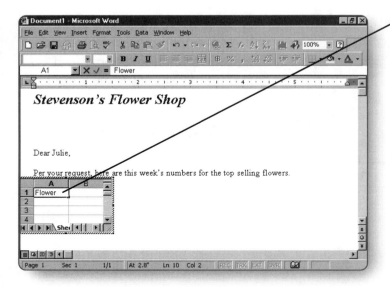

7. **Enter** the **data** you want to appear in that cell.

8. **Press** the **Enter key**. Excel will accept the data and move to the next cell.

TIP

If you accidentally click outside the Excel worksheet and the Excel screen disappears and the Word screen appears, double-click inside the worksheet, and the Excel screen will reappear.

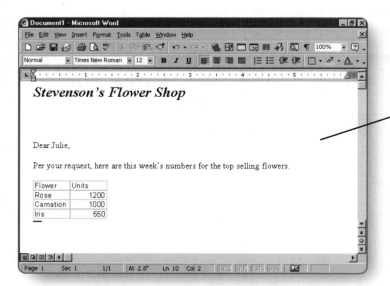

9. **Repeat steps 6** through **8** until you have entered all the data you want in the worksheet and formatted it.

10. **Click** on an **area** outside the worksheet to see how it will look in the Word document. The Excel screen will disappear, and the Word screen will reappear.

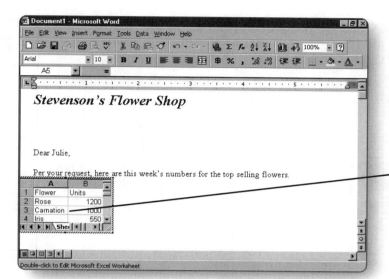

Formatting the New Excel Worksheet

You can change the number category, font, and alignment of the Excel worksheet, using the Excel Format menu.

1. Double-click in the **Excel worksheet** area. The Excel controls will appear.

2. Click on **Format**. The Format menu will appear.

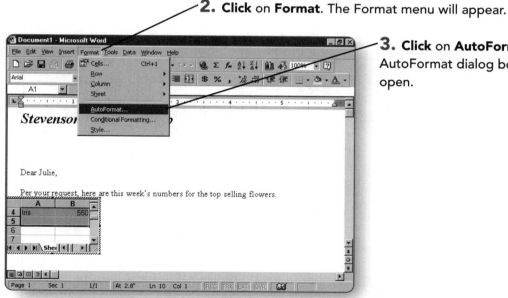

3. Click on **AutoFormat**. The AutoFormat dialog box will open.

4. Click on a **format** that you want to use.

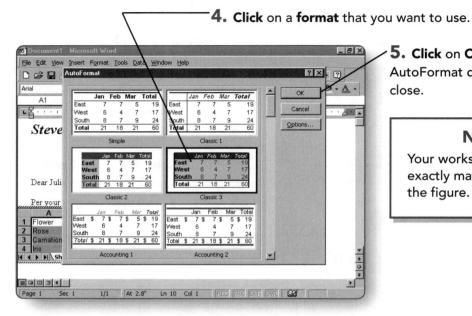

5. Click on **OK**. The AutoFormat dialog box will close.

NOTE

Your worksheet may not exactly match the one in the figure.

6. Click on an **area** outside the worksheet to see how it will look in the Word document. The Excel screen will disappear, and the Word screen will appear with the formatted Excel worksheet.

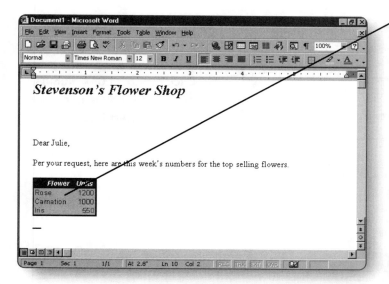

The worksheet will appear in the format that you chose.

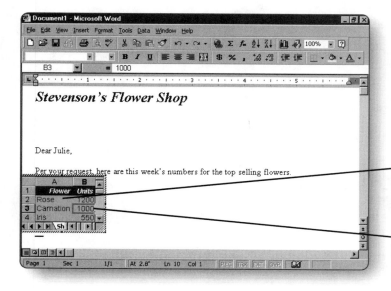

Inserting Rows or Columns in the Excel Worksheet

If you forget a row or column, you can use the Excel window to insert the missing element.

1. **Double-click** in the **Excel worksheet**. The Excel screen will appear.

2. **Click** in the **cell** where you want the new element to appear. The cell will be selected.

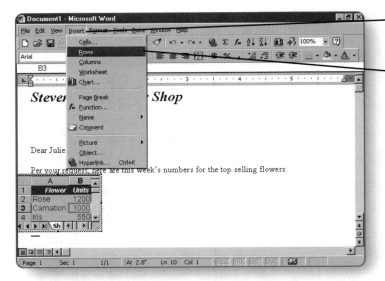

3. Click on **Insert**. The Insert menu will appear.

4. Click on **Rows** or **Columns**, depending on the element that you want to insert into the worksheet.

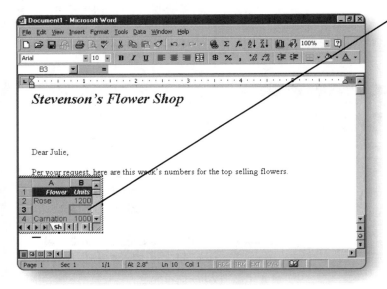

The new row or column will be inserted.

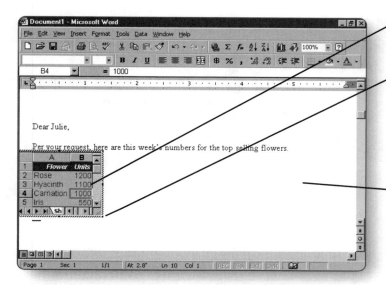

5. **Enter** the **data** that is missing.

6. **Drag** the **selection handles** of the Excel worksheet. The worksheet will expand so that you can see all rows and columns.

7. **Click outside** the Excel worksheet. The Excel screen will disappear, and you will be able to continue typing and complete the Word document.

Inserting an Existing Excel Worksheet into Word

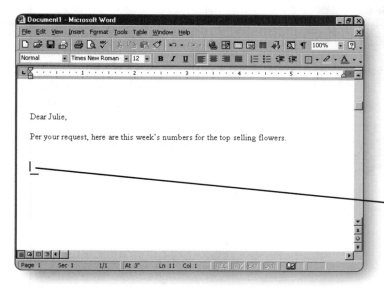

You also can insert entire existing Excel worksheets into Word documents, embedding the worksheets or linking them. *Linking files* means that changes you make in the worksheet in the Excel file also appear in the Word file that contains the Excel worksheet.

1. **Click** in the **Word document** where you want your Excel worksheet to appear. The insertion point will be placed.

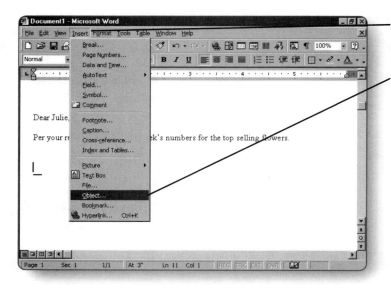

2. Click on **Insert**. The Insert menu will appear.

3. Click on **Object**. The Object dialog box will open.

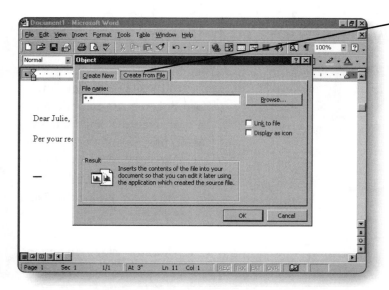

4. Click on the **Create from File tab**. The tab will come to the front.

NOTE

If you can't remember the filename, use the Browse button.

5. Type the **filename** of the Excel worksheet in the File name: text box.

6. Click on either or both of the following **check box options** that you want to use with this worksheet. A ✔ will appear in the box next to the option(s) chosen.

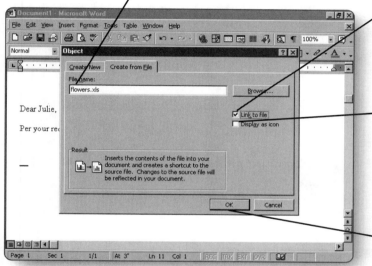

- If you use the Link to file option, the worksheet in the Word document changes whenever the Excel file changes.

- If you use the Display as icon option, an icon will appear in your Word document, not the actual worksheet. The reader then clicks on the icon to open the worksheet.

7. Click on **OK**. The Object dialog box will close, and the worksheet will appear in your document.

Linking a Part of an Existing Excel Sheet

If you want to link only certain cells from an Excel sheet, you must use the Paste Special command.

1. In Word, **position** the **insertion point** where you want the Excel cells to appear.

2. Click the **Minimize button**. The Word screen will be minimized.

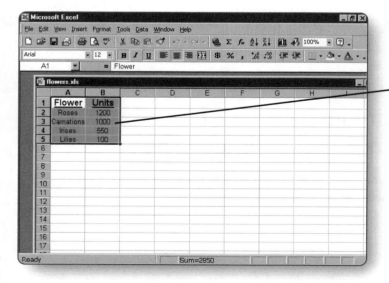

3. In Excel, **open** the **workbook** from which you want to link cells.

4. Drag across the **cells** you want to select. The cells will be selected.

5. Click on **Edit**. The Edit menu will appear.

6. Click on **Copy**. The cells will be copied to the Clipboard.

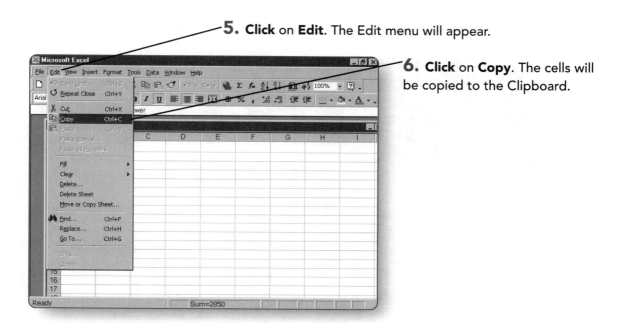

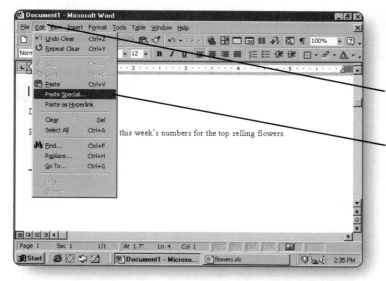

7. Click on **Word** in the Windows Taskbar. The Word window will reopen.

8. Click on **Edit**. The Edit menu will appear.

9. Click on **Paste Special**. The Paste Special dialog box will open.

10. **Click** on **Paste link**. The item will be selected.

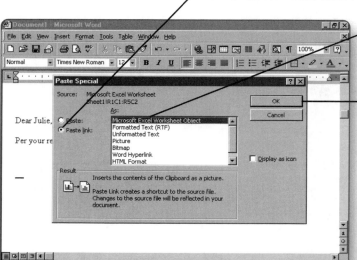

11. **Click** on **Microsoft Excel Worksheet Object** in the As: list. The item will be selected.

12. **Click** on **OK**. The cells will be pasted into your Word document.

TIP

By choosing Paste Link in step 10, you create a link between the original Excel file and the Word file so that when the Excel copy changes, the Word copy will too. If you don't want that, choose Paste in step 10 instead, or simply choose the Paste command instead of Paste Special in step 9.

Part V Review Questions

1. What are some of the statistical functions that Excel offers? *See "Working with Statistical Functions" in Chapter 18*

2. How can you use the FV function in your finances? *See "Working with Financial Functions" in Chapter 18*

3. What does the term "depreciation" mean? *See the introduction in Chapter 19*

4. What function calculates straight line depreciation? *See "Calculating the Straight Line Depreciation" in Chapter 19*

5. What information does an amortization table provide? *See the introduction in Chapter 20*

6. What functions calculate the interest, principal, and payment amounts of a loan? *See the introduction in Chapter 20*

7. What is an advantage to having a word processing program and a spreadsheet program that are compatible? *See the introduction in Chapter 21*

8. What limitations does embedding an object within a document create? *See "Creating an Excel Worksheet from Within Word" in Chapter 21*

9. How can you quickly create an Excel worksheet within a Word document? *See "Creating an Excel Worksheet from Within Word" in Chapter 21*

10. What does the term "linking" files mean? *See "Inserting an Existing Excel Worksheet into Word" in Chapter 21*

Getting Online with Excel

22

Excel and the Internet

Many of Microsoft Office 2000's major improvements over earlier versions lie in the area of Internet usage. With Excel 2000, Microsoft has made it much easier for the average person to publish data on the Internet in an attractive and usable format. In this chapter, you'll learn how to:

- Insert a hyperlink
- Create an e-mail link
- Save an Excel worksheet in Web format
- Provide editable worksheets to Web users

Inserting a Hyperlink

As you may already know from exploring the Internet, many Web pages contain underlined strings of text that you can click on to jump to a specific Web page. These are called *hyperlinks*. A hyperlink can be text in a cell, or it can be attached to any other object, such as a picture, map, or graph.

Even if you are not planning to save your Excel workbook in Web format, you might still want to include hyperlinks in it. For example, a hyperlink can provide a cross-reference to more information on a particular topic.

1. **Click** on the **cell** where you want to insert the hyperlink, or select the graphic, map, or chart.

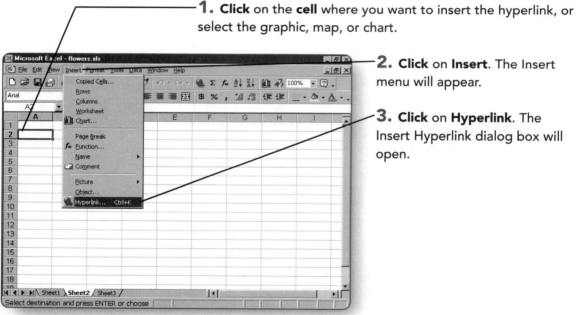

2. **Click** on **Insert**. The Insert menu will appear.

3. **Click** on **Hyperlink**. The Insert Hyperlink dialog box will open.

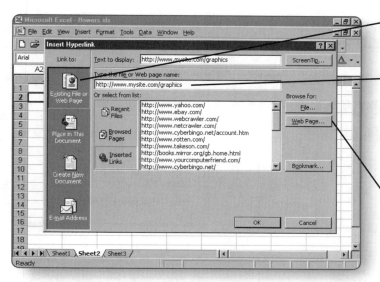

4. Click on **Existing File or Web Page** in the Link to: list.

5a. Type the **address** of the Web page in the Type the file or Web page name: box and skip to step 8.

OR

5b. Click on the **Web Page button** to browse for the Web page. Your Web browser program will open.

6. Navigate in your **Web browser** to the page to which you want to link.

NOTE

You can use your Favorites list to choose a favorite page, or follow hyperlinks from your Start page to get to the page you want.

7. Click on **Excel** on the Taskbar to switch back to Excel. The page's address will be filled in for you.

8. Type the text that you want to display in the Text to display: box if the desired text does not already appear there.

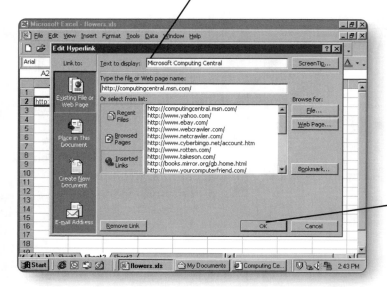

NOTE

The text you type in step 8 will be the underlined text that appears in the cell. If you type nothing here, the actual address will be used for the text.

9. Click on **OK**. The hyperlink will appear in the cell.

If you attached the hyperlink to an object, it may not be immediately obvious that it's there, but the next two steps will confirm its presence.

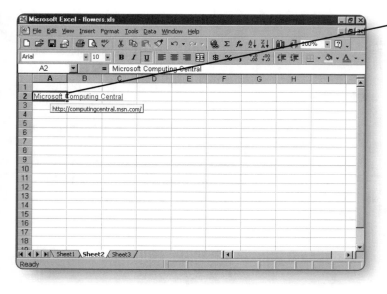

10. Point your **mouse** at the cell or object. A ScreenTip will appear showing the actual address.

11. Click on the **hyperlink**. Your Web browser will open and display the page.

Inserting an E-Mail Link

You can include a hyperlink that, instead of jumping to a Web page, opens a window in which an e-mail message can be composed and sent. This is handy if you want readers of your worksheet to be able to e-mail questions and comments to a certain person.

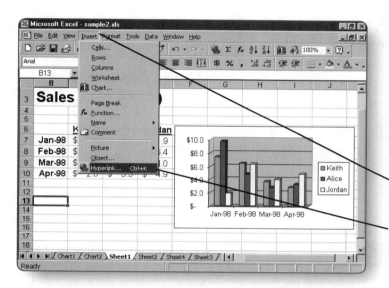

1. Click on the **cell** where you want the hyperlink to appear. The cell will be highlighted.

2. Click on **Insert**. The Insert menu will appear.

3. Click on **Hyperlink**. The Insert Hyperlink dialog box will open.

4. Click on **E-mail Address** in the Link to: list.

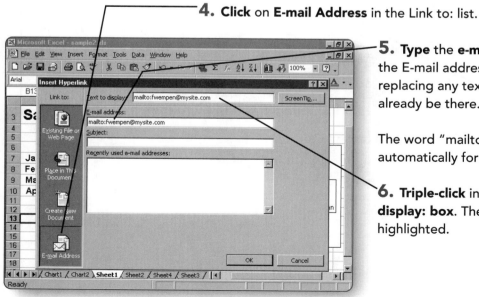

5. Type the **e-mail address** in the E-mail address: box, replacing any text that may already be there.

The word "mailto:" is filled in automatically for you.

6. Triple-click in the **Text to display: box**. The text will be highlighted.

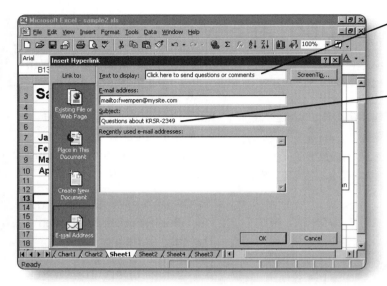

7. **Type instructions** for the link. The instructions will appear in the Text to display: box.

8. **Click** in the **Subject: box**. The insertion point will move there.

9. **Type** a **subject** for the e-mails to be sent.

10. **Click** on **OK**. The link will be created.

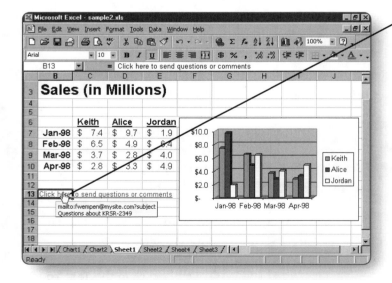

11. **Point** your **mouse** at the cell or object. A ScreenTip will appear showing the actual address.

12. **Click** on the **hyperlink**. Your default e-mail program will open, displaying a new e-mail window.

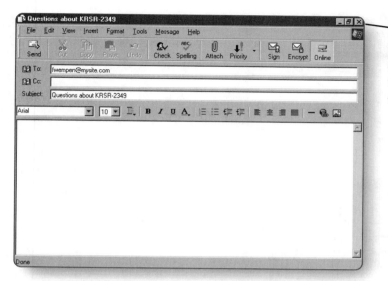

13. **Click** on **Close button** (X). The e-mail program will close. (You don't actually want to send a message; we are just testing the link.)

Saving the Worksheet for the Web

When you save your worksheet in Web format, you make it possible for others who do not have Excel to view your data. All they need is a Web browser program.

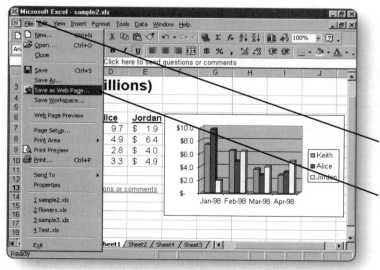

1. (Optional) **Select** the **range of cells** to save in Web format.

Do step 1 only if you do not want the entire active sheet or the entire workbook.

2. **Click** on **File**. The File menu will appear.

3. **Click** on **Save as Web Page**. The Save As dialog box will open.

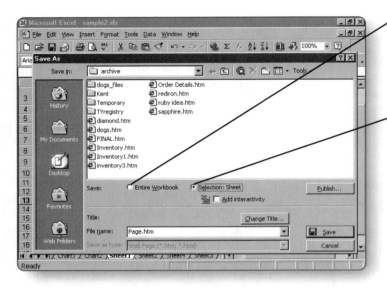

4a. **Click** on **Entire Workbook** to save the entire workbook (all sheets).

OR

4b. **Click** on **Selection** to save the selection.

If you did not select cells in step 1, the Selection is the sheet.

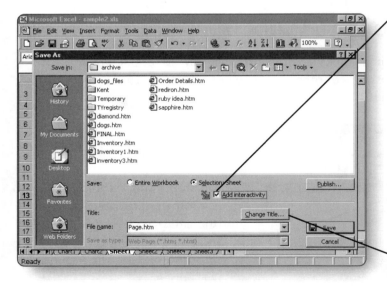

5. (Optional) **Click** on **Add interactivity**. A ✔ will appear in the box.

Do this if you want the reader to be able to work with the data (for example, search it or sort it). Be aware, however, that if you choose to add interactivity, you will lose all the non-cell objects on the sheet. That means that no maps or charts will appear.

6. Click on **Change Title**. The Set Title dialog box will open.

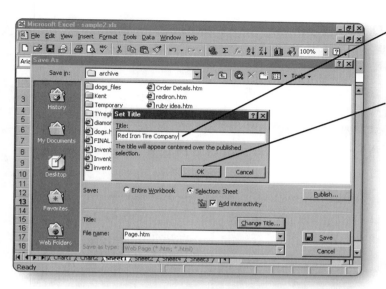

7. **Type** the **title** that you want to appear in the title bar when the Web page is displayed.

8. **Click** on **OK**. The Set Title dialog box will close.

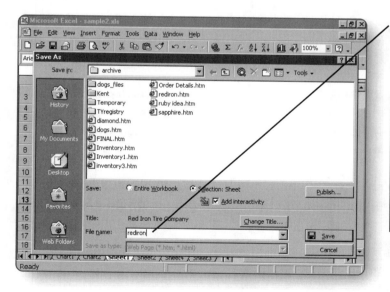

9. **Type** a **filename** in the File name: box. This name will be part of the page's Web address.

NOTE

You do not have to type .htm or .html at the end of the name in step 9; Excel will add that for you automatically.

10a. **Click** on **Save**. The page will be saved.

OR

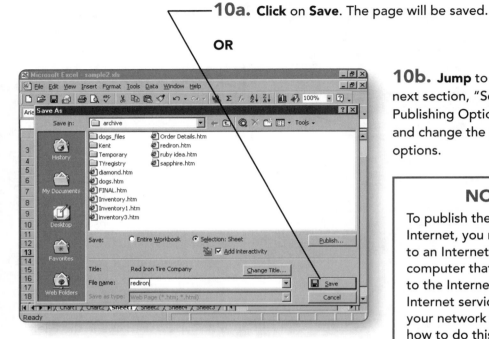

10b. **Jump** to the **steps** in the next section, "Setting More Publishing Options," to view and change the publishing options.

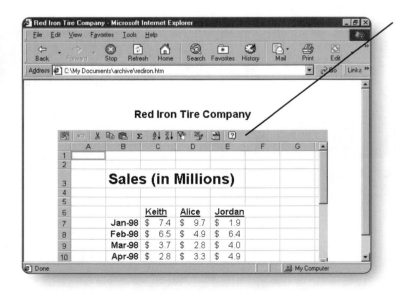

When your reader displays the page in a Web browser, if you chose to include user interactivity in step 5, the controls appear as shown here. Pointing the mouse pointer at each tool provides a ScreenTip that explains the tool's purpose.

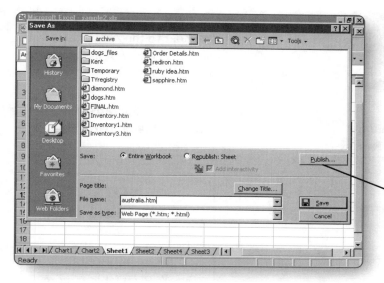

Setting More Publishing Options

Instead of clicking Save in step 10 of the previous section, you can do the following.

1. Click on **Publish**. The Publish as Web Page dialog box will open.

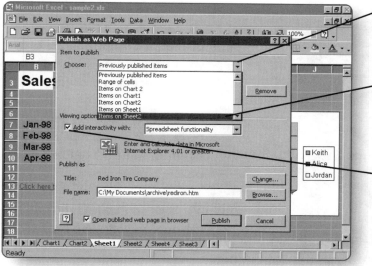

2. Click on the **down arrow** (▼) next to Choose:. A list of options will appear.

3. Click on a **different item** to publish if desired. All the items from all the sheets in the workbook will appear.

4a. Select the **Add interactivity with: check box** if you want interactivity. A ✔ will appear in the box.

OR

4b. If you don't want interactivity, make sure that it is *not* marked, and then **skip** to **step 7**.

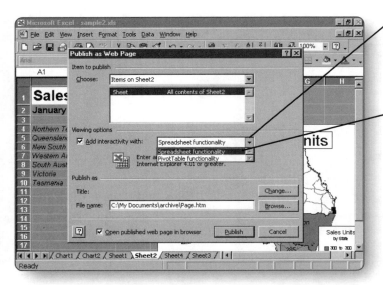

5. Click on the **down arrow** (▼) next to the Add interactivity with: check box. A list of options will appear.

6. Click on **Spreadsheet functionality** or **PivotTable functionality**.

NOTE
PivotTable functionality gives the reader the ability to analyze the published data using Excel's PivotTable feature.

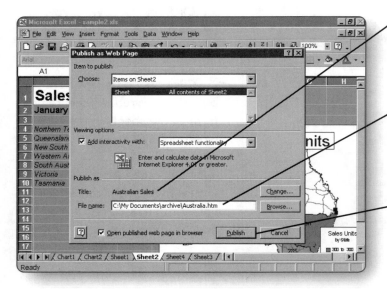

7. Confirm that the **Title** is correct. If it is not, change it, as you learned in steps 6 through 8 of the preceding procedure.

8. Confirm that the **Filename** is correct. If it is not, type a different name in the File name: box.

9. Click on **Publish**. The page will open in your Web browser, for your inspection.

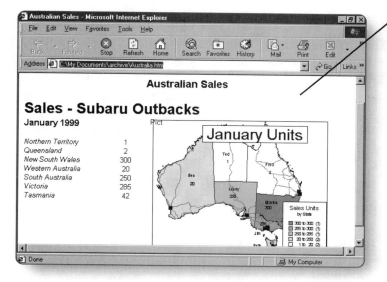

This page, which contains a map, appears in Internet Explorer. If this page had been published with user interactivity, the map would not show up. This is the sacrifice you make for the added functionality.

Viewing a Web Page

If you use the publishing options from the preceding steps, your Web browser opens automatically. But you can also open the Web browser manually and open a page for viewing.

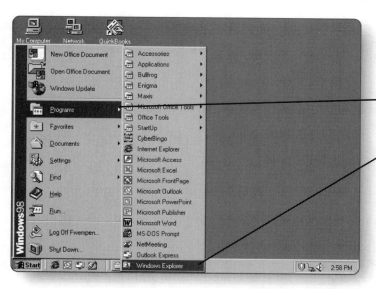

1. Click on **Start** from the Windows desktop. The Start menu will appear.

2. Click on **Programs**. The Programs menu will appear.

3. Click on **Windows Explorer**. The Windows Explorer dialog box will open.

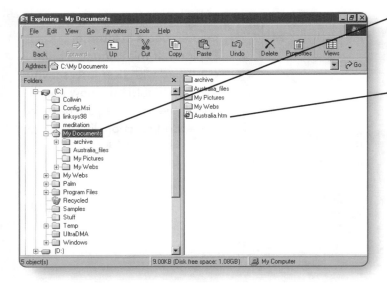

4. Click on the **folder** where the file is stored. By default it is My Documents.

5. Double-click on the **file**. The file will open in Internet Explorer (or your default Web browser, if different).

Part VI Review Questions

1. What happens when the reader of a worksheet clicks on a hyperlink? *See "Inserting a Hyperlink" in Chapter 22*

2. What kinds of objects can you attach a hyperlink to? *See "Inserting a Hyperlink" in Chapter 22*

3. What happens when the reader of a worksheet clicks on an e-mail link? *See "Inserting an E-Mail Link" in Chapter 22*

4. What command on the File menu is used to save a worksheet in Web format? *See "Saving the Worksheet for the Web" in Chapter 22*

PART VII

Appendixes

A

Office 2000 Installation

Installing Office 2000 is typically very quick and easy. In this appendix, you'll learn how to:

- Install Office 2000 on your computer
- Choose which Office components you want to install
- Detect and repair problems
- Reinstall Office
- Add and remove components
- Uninstall Office 2000 completely
- Install content from other Office CDs

Installing the Software

The installation program for the Office 2000 programs is automatic. In most cases, you can simply follow the instructions onscreen.

NOTE

When you insert the Office 2000 CD for the first time, you may see a message that the installer has been updated, prompting you to restart your system. Do so, and when you return to Windows after restarting, remove the CD and reinsert it so that the Setup program starts up automatically again.

---

1. Insert the **Office 2000 CD-ROM** into your computer's CD-ROM drive. The Windows Installer will start and the Customer Information dialog box will open.

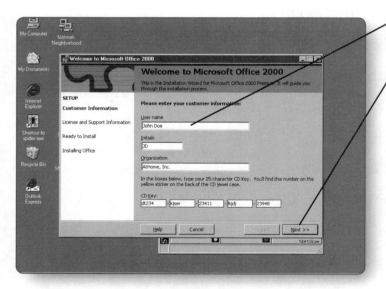

2. Type all of the **information** requested.

3. Click on **Next**. The End User License Agreement will appear.

NOTE

You'll find the CD Key number on a sticker on the back of the Office CD jewel case.

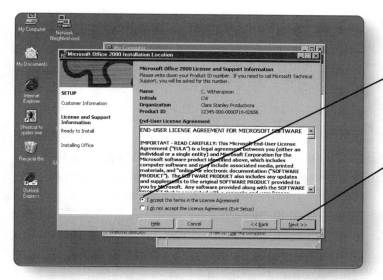

4. Read the **License Agreement**.

5. Click on the **I accept the terms in the License Agreement option button**. The option will be selected.

6. Click on **Next**. The Ready To Install dialog box will open.

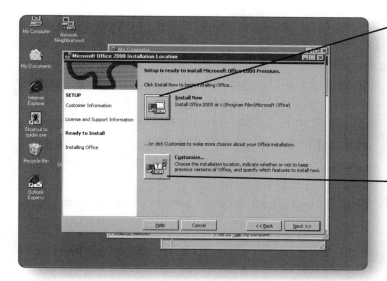

7a. Click on the **Install Now button.** Use this option to install Office on your computer with the default settings. This is the recommended installation for most users.

OR

7b. Click on the **Customize button**, if you want to choose which components to install or where to install them. The Installation Location dialog box will open. Then see the next section, "Choosing Components," for guidance.

8. Wait while the **Office software** installs on your computer. When the setup has completed, the Installer Information box will open.

9. Click on **Yes**. The Setup Wizard will restart your computer. After your computer has restarted, Windows will update your system settings and then finish the Office installation and configuration process.

Choosing Components

If you selected option 7b in the previous section, you have the choice of installing many different programs and components.

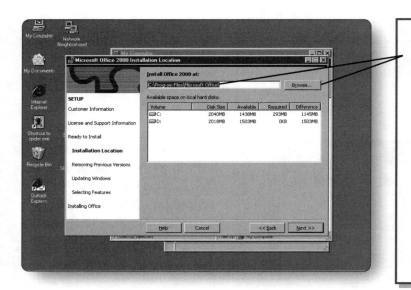

NOTE

For a custom installation, you have the option of placing Office in a different location on your computer. It is recommended that you use the default installation location. If you want to install Office in a different directory, type the directory path in the text box or click on the Browse button to select a directory.

1. Click on **Next**. The Selecting Features dialog box will open.

2. Click on a **plus sign (+)** to expand a list of features. The features listed under the category will appear.

3. Click on the **down arrow (▼)** to the right of the hard drive icon. A menu of available installation options for the feature will appear.

4. Click on the **button** next to the individual option, and choose a setting for that option:

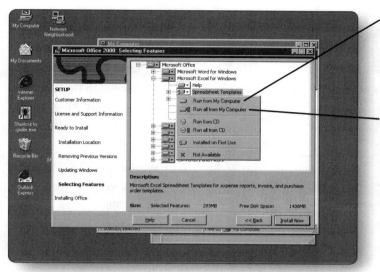

- **Run from My Computer**. The component will be fully installed, so that you will not need the Office CD in the CD-ROM drive to use it.

- **Run all from My Computer**. The selected component and all the components subordinate to it will be fully installed.

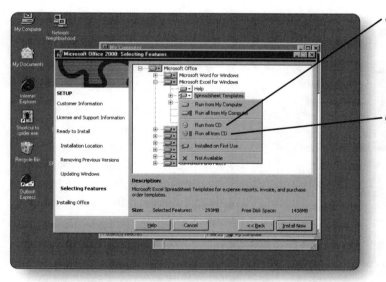

- **Run from CD**. The component will be installed, but you will need to have the Office CD in the CD-ROM drive to use it.

- **Run all from CD**. The selected component and all the components subordinate to it will need to have the Office CD in the CD-ROM drive to use it.

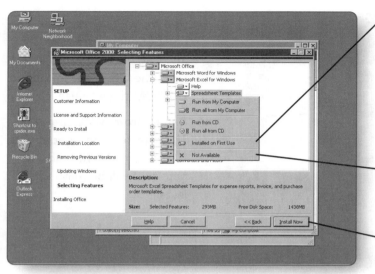

• **Installed on First Use**. The first time you try to activate the component, you will be prompted to insert the Office CD to fully install it. This is good for components that you are not sure whether you will need or not.

• **Not Available**. The component will not be installed at all.

5. Click on **Install Now**. The Installing dialog box will open.

In a Custom installation, you'll be asked whether you want to update Internet Explorer to version 5.0. Your choices are:

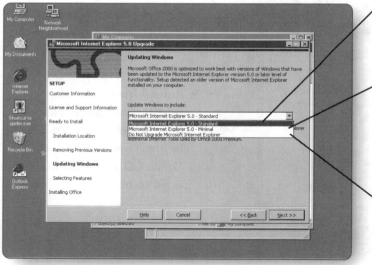

• **Microsoft Internet Explorer 5.0—Standard**. This is the default, and the right choice for most people.

• **Microsoft Internet Explorer 5.0—Minimal**. This is the right choice if you are running out of hard disk space but still would like to use Internet Explorer 5.0.

• **Do Not Upgrade Microsoft Internet Explorer**. Use this if you don't want Internet Explorer (for example, if you always use another browser such as Netscape Navigator, or if you have been directed by your system administrator not to install Internet Explorer 5).

Working with Maintenance Mode

Maintenance Mode is a feature of the Setup program. Whenever you run the Setup program again, after the initial installation, Maintenance Mode starts automatically. It enables you to add or remove features, repair your Office installation (for example, if files have become corrupted), and remove Office completely. There are several ways to rerun the Setup program (and thus enter Maintenance Mode):

- Reinsert the Office 2000 CD. The Setup program may start automatically.

- If the Setup program does not start automatically, double-click on the CD icon in the My Computer window.

- If double-clicking on the CD icon doesn't work, right-click on the CD icon and click on Open from the shortcut menu. Then double-click on the Setup.exe file in the list of files that appears.

- From the Control Panel in Windows, click on the Add/ Remove Programs button. Then on the Install/Uninstall tab, click on Microsoft Office 2000 in the list, and finally, click on the Add/Remove button.

After entering Maintenance Mode, choose the button for the activity you want. Each option is briefly described in the following sections.

Repairing or Reinstalling Office

If an Office program is behaving strangely, or refuses to work, chances are good that a needed file has become corrupted. But which file? You have no way of knowing, so you can't fix the problem yourself.

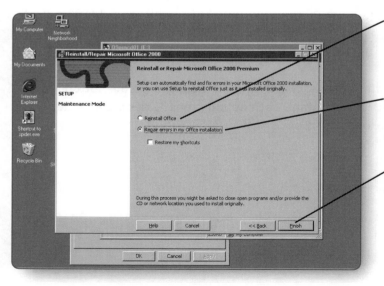

If this happens, you can either repair Office or completely reinstall it. Both options are accessed from the Repair Office button in Maintenance Mode.

1. Click on the **Repair Office button** in Maintenance Mode.

2a. Click on **Reinstall Office** to repeat the last installation.

OR

2b. Click on Repair errors in my Office installation to simply fix what's already in place.

3. Click on **Finish**. The process will start.

TIP

You can also repair individual Office programs by opening the Help menu in each program and clicking on Detect and Repair. This works well if you are sure that one certain program is causing the problem, and it's quicker than asking the Setup program to check all of the installed programs.

Adding and Removing Components

Adding and removing components works just like selecting the components initially.

1. Click on the **Add or Remove Features button** in Maintenance Mode. The Update Features window will appear. This window works exactly the same as the window you saw in the "Choosing Components" section earlier in this appendix.

NOTE

Some features will attempt to automatically install themselves as you are working. If you have set a feature to be installed on first use, attempt to access that feature. You will be prompted to insert your Office 2000 CD, and the feature will be installed without further prompting.

Removing Office from Your PC

In the unlikely event that you should need to remove Office from your PC completely, click on Remove Office from the Maintenance Mode screen. Then follow the prompts to remove it from your system.

After removing Office, you will probably have a few remnants left behind that the Uninstall routine didn't catch. For example, there will probably still be a Microsoft Office folder in your Program Files folder or wherever you installed the program. You can delete that folder yourself.

CAUTION

If you plan to reinstall Office later, and you have created any custom templates, toolbars, or other items, you may want to leave the Microsoft Office folder alone, so that those items will be available to you after you reinstall.

Installing Content from Other Office CDs

Depending on the version of Office you bought, you may have more than one CD in your package. CD 1 contains all the basic Office components, such as Word, Outlook, PowerPoint, Excel, Access, and Internet Explorer. It may be the only CD you need to use.

The other CDs contain extra applications that come with the specific version of Office you purchased. They may include Publisher, FrontPage, a language pack, or a programmer and developer resource kit. Each of these discs has its own separate installation program.

The additional CDs should start their Setup programs automatically when you insert the disc in your drive. If not, browse the CD's content in My Computer or Windows Explorer and double-click on the Setup.exe file that you find on it.

B

Using Keyboard Shortcuts

Keyboard shortcuts are key combinations you can press as alternatives to choosing menu commands, selecting text or ranges, or applying certain formatting. You may have also noticed keyboard shortcuts listed next to certain menu commands.

For a complete list of keyboard shortcuts, check out the Excel 2000 Help system. This appendix provides a few of the most common ones to get you started.

When several keys are listed together, you hold down the first key(s) while tapping the second. For example, if you see Shift+F1, hold down the Shift key, tap F1, and then release Shift.

Getting Help

Find out more about using Excel through the Help system with these keyboard shortcuts:

To Do This	Press This
Summon the Office Assistant	F1
Get What's This? help on-screen elements	Shift+F1

Working with Menus

Ever wondered about the underlined letters on menu and command names? Those are *selection letters*, and they exist so that you can work with menus and commands using the following shortcuts:

To Do This	Press This
Open a menu	Alt, and then the menu's selection letter
Select a menu command	Up and down arrow keys, and then Enter, or the menu item's selection letter
Close a menu or dialog box	Esc
Show a shortcut menu	Shift+F10

Opening Dialog Boxes

Some of the most common dialog boxes have their own shortcuts, so you can bypass their menu commands:

To Open This Dialog Box	Press This
Save As	Shift+F12
	(Ctrl+S also opens it if the file has not been saved before)
Format Cells	Ctrl+1
Print	Ctrl+P
Go To	F5
Open	Ctrl+O
Spelling	F7
Find	Shift+F5

Moving Around in a Worksheet or Workbook

To move the cell cursor around in the workbook, or scroll from one part of the workbook to another, use these shortcuts:

To Move	Press This
One cell in any direction	An arrow key
One screenful in any direction	Alt+ an arrow key
To the edge of the current data region	Ctrl+ an arrow key
To the beginning of the current row	Home
To the top of the worksheet (cell A1)	Ctrl+Home
Up or down one screenful	Page Up and Page Down
To the next cell (right)	Tab
To the previous cell (left)	Shift+Tab

Typing Data into Cells

When you are typing data, you can save time with these:

To Do This	Press This
Start a new formula	= (equal sign)
Start an AutoSum	Alt+= (equal sign)
Start a new line in the same cell	Alt+Enter
Move the insertion point	Arrow keys
Copy the formula from the cell above	Ctrl+' (apostrophe)
Insert today's date	Ctrl+; (semi-colon)
Copy the value from the cell above	Ctrl+Shift+" (quotation mark)
Insert the current time	Ctrl+Shift+: (colon)
Cancel entry in a cell	Esc

Applying Number Formats

Many of the number formats (from the Number tab of the Format Cells dialog box) can be applied with keyboard shortcuts:

To Apply This Format	Press This
Number	Ctrl+Shift+!
Date	Ctrl+Shift+#
Currency	Ctrl+Shift+$
Percentage	Ctrl+Shift+%
Time	Ctrl+Shift+@
Exponential	Ctrl+Shift+^
General	Ctrl+Shift+~

Formatting Data

The most popular text formatting commands (bold, italic, and underline) not only have their own toolbar buttons, but their own keyboard shortcuts too.

To Do This	Press This
Turn Bold on and off	Ctrl+B
Turn Italics on and off	Ctrl+I
Turn Underline on and off	Ctrl+U
Open the Format Cells dialog box	Ctrl+1

Selecting Ranges of Cells

To select multiple cells, you can use these keyboard shortcuts instead of the usual mouse-dragging method:

To Do This	Press This
Select the entire worksheet	Ctrl+A
Extend the selection	Shift+arrow key
Extend the selection to the end of the row or column	Ctrl+Shift+arrow key Ctrl+Shift+arrow key
Extend the selection to the bottommost, rightmost cell containing data in the sheet	Ctrl+Shift+End Ctrl+Shift+End
Extend the selection to cell A1	Ctrl+Shift+Home
Select the column	Ctrl+Spacebar
Extend the selection to the beginning of the row	Shift+Home
Select the row	Shift+Spacebar

Cutting, Copying, and Pasting

Once you've selected a range, you can cut, copy, paste, delete, or clear it. Not only do you have the Edit menu's commands for these actions, and the toolbar buttons, but also these keyboard shortcuts:

To Do This	Press This
Cut the selection	Ctrl+X
Copy the selection	Ctrl+C
Paste the selection	Ctrl+V
Delete the selection	Ctrl+- (hyphen)
Clear the contents of the selection	Delete

Glossary

+. Addition operator.

-. Subtraction operator.

=. Initiates all formulas.

*. Multiplication operator.

/. Division operator.

>. Greater than operator.

<. Less than operator.

<>. Not equal to operator.

:. Range operator.

A

Absolute reference. References to cell addresses that don't change based on where a formula is located in a worksheet.

Active cell. The selected cell in a worksheet.

Address. A named reference to a cell based on its location at the intersection of a column and row; for example, the cell in the fourth row of the second column has an address of B4.

Alignment. The arrangement of text or an object in relation to the document's margins in Word, a slide's dimensions in PowerPoint, or a cell's edges in Excel. Alignment can be left, right, centered, or justified.

Array. A contiguous set of cells in a worksheet.

AutoFormat. Predefined sets of styles that allow you to quickly apply formatting (color, font, and so on) to your Excel worksheet.

AutoSum. A built-in addition function that allows you to add a row or column of figures using the AutoSum button on the Excel toolbar.

Axis (pl. axes). In a graph, one of two value sets (*see also* **Y-axis** and **X-axis**).

B

Bar chart. A type of chart that uses bars of varying lengths to represent values.

Border. A formatting option that places a line around any of the four sides of an object, such as a cell.

C

Cell. The area defined by a rectangle at which a row and column intersect in an Excel worksheet.

Cell reference. A method of referring to a cell in a formula by listing the location of its row and column intersection.

Chart. Also called *graph*. A chart is a visual representation of numerical data.

Circular reference. In a formula, a circular reference indicates that a calculation should return to its starting point and repeat endlessly; a circular reference in a formula results in an error message.

Clip art. Ready-made line drawings that are included with Office in the Clip Art Gallery; these drawings can be inserted into Office documents.

Column. A set of cells running vertically down a worksheet.

Combination chart. A chart that uses more than one style of representing data; for example, bars for one set of data and a line for another set of data. A chart that shows rainfall in a country by month with bars and the average rainfall in the world with a line is an example of a combination chart.

D

Data. Information, which can be either numerical or textual.

Data series. In charts, elements that represent a set of data, such as pie segment, line, or bar.

Data type. The category of numerical data, such as currency, scientific, or percentage.

Desktop. Windows' main work area.

Drag-and-drop. A feature that allows you to move an object or selected text around an Excel worksheet using your mouse.

E

Equation. *See* **Formula**.

F

Fill. A function that allows Excel to automatically complete a series of numbers based on an established pattern.

Fill (color). A formatting feature used to apply color or a pattern to the interior of an object, such as a cell.

Fill handle. A block at the bottom-right corner of all cells in a worksheet that is used to fill cells as it is dragged across with a pattern of data.

Filter. To make settings so that only cells that meet certain criteria are displayed in your worksheet.

Financial functions. Functions (stored formulas) that are used with money, such as payments and interest rates.

Flip. To turn an object on a page 180 degrees.

Font. A design family of text, also called a *typeface*.

Footer. Text repeated at the bottom of each page of a document.

Format. To apply settings for font, color, size, and style to data or objects.

Formula. An equation that instructs Excel to perform certain calculations based on numerical data in designated cells.

Formula bar. The location where all data and formulas are entered for a selected cell.

Freezing. In large worksheets, it is sometimes desirable to freeze a portion of the sheet, such as column headings, so that it doesn't scroll off screen when you move down the page.

Function. A predefined, named formula.

G

General format. A numerical type applied to numbers in cells.

Goal Seek. A feature that allows you to enter the result you want. Excel then determines changes in the formula or data required to obtain the result.

Go To. A feature of Excel that allows you to move quickly to a page or cell of your worksheet based on criteria you provide.

Graphs. *See* **Chart**.

Greater than. A function that restricts a number result to be higher than a named number.

Gridlines. Lines between the cells of a worksheet, which can be displayed and printed or not.

H

Header. Text repeated at the top of each page of a document.

Hide. A feature of Excel that allows you to temporarily stop displaying designated cells in a worksheet.

I

Icon. In software, a picture representing a feature, such as tool button icon.

IF function. A predefined formula indicating that a result is to occur only if some criteria is met. For example, you could use this function to indicate that "if the result of a sum is greater than 10, the result should appear in this cell."

J

Justify. To space a line of text across a cell evenly from the left margin to the right margin.

L

Label. A descriptive text element added to a chart to help the reader understand a visual element. Also refers to row or column headings.

Landscape. A page orientation that prints a document with the long edge of the paper across the top.

Legend. A definition of the various elements of a chart or graph.

Less than. A predefined function that indicates a result should occur only if a number is less than the specified number.

Logical functions. Functions that are based on the logical consequence of a named set of circumstances, such as the IF . . . THEN function.

M

Macro. A saved series of keystrokes that can be played back to perform an action.

Maps. Representing data in charts with geographical maps rather than traditional chart elements such as bars and lines.

Mathematical functions. Functions that produce mathematical results, such as SUM and AVG.

N

Name definitions. Providing an alternate name for a cell so that you can use that name definition in formulas.

Named ranges. Providing a name for a set of cells so you can use that name in formulas.

O

Object. A picture, map, or other graphic element that you can place in an Excel worksheet.

Office Assistant. A help feature for Microsoft Office products that allows you to ask questions in standard English sentence format.

Operator. The parts of a formula that indicate an action to be performed, such as addition (+) or division (/).

Optional arguments. A portion of a formula which is not necessary to achieve the result, but that designates an action other than the default. An optional argument to include decimals in a result would include the decimal point and two zeros even if the number doesn't contain cents.

Orientation. The way a document prints on a piece of paper; landscape prints with the longer side of a page on top, while portrait prints with the shorter edge at the top.

P

Passwords. A word selected by an Excel user to protect a worksheet; after a sheet is protected, the correct password must be entered to modify that sheet.

Paste. To insert an object or text placed on the Windows Clipboard into a document.

Patterns. Predefined shading and line arrangements used to format cells in a worksheet.

Pie chart. A round chart type in which each pie wedge represents a value.

Plot. The area of a chart where data is drawn using elements such as lines, bars, or pie wedges.

Portrait. A page orientation where a document prints with the shorter edge of the paper along the top.

Precedent. Some formulas call on data that is the result of another formula; the precedent is the formula that originally created the data being named in the second formula.

Print area. The portion of a worksheet you designate to print.

Print Preview. A feature that allows you to view a document on your screen appearing as it will when printed.

Protection. To make settings to a worksheet so that only those authorized can modify the worksheet.

R

Range. A collection of cells, ranging from the first named cell to the last.

Recalculation. Used with manual calculation, recalculation is applied to a formula when data has changed to receive the new result.

Redo. A feature of Excel that allows you to repeat an action you have reversed using the Undo feature.

Reference. In a formula, a name or range that refers the formula to a cell or set of cells.

Relative. In a formula, making reference to a cell relative to the location of the cell where the formula is placed; if the formula cell is moved, the cell being referenced changes in relation to the new location.

Rotate. To manipulate an object so that it moves around a 360-degree axis.

Row. A set of cells running from left to right across a worksheet.

S

Save as. To save a previously saved worksheet with a new name or properties.

Scroll bar. A device used to move up and down or left to right in a worksheet to display various portions of it onscreen.

Shading. A gray to black pattern used to format cells in a worksheet.

Sheet. *See* **Worksheet**.

Sort. To arrange information in a column or row alphanumerically, in ascending or descending order.

Spelling. A feature of Excel that verifies the spelling of words in your worksheets.

Spreadsheet. A software program used to perform calculations on data.

Style. A saved, named set of formatting such as color, size, and font that can be applied to data in a worksheet.

SUM function. A saved, named function of addition that can be applied to cells by typing the term "SUM" in a formula.

Syntax. The structure and order of the functions and references used in a formula.

T

Target cell. The cell where the results of a formula should be placed.

Template. A predefined set of worksheet formats included with Excel that are useful for quickly generating certain types of documents, such as an invoice.

Text box. A text object that you can create with the drawing feature of Excel to place text anywhere on a chart or worksheet; often used to label elements of a chart or worksheet.

Titles. Names of the elements of a chart.

U

Undo. An Excel feature that allows you to reverse the last action performed.

Unhide. To reveal cells previously hidden in a worksheet.

Unprotect. To remove password safeguards from a worksheet so that anyone can modify the worksheet.

V

Value. Another term for a number.

Variable. Cells that are changed to see what results from that change.

W

What if. A scenario in a formula that supposes certain criteria.

What's This?. A part of the Excel Help system; once you select What's This? your cursor changes to a question mark and you can click on any onscreen element to receive an explanation of that element.

Wizard. A feature of Excel that walks you through a procedure step by step; a wizard creates something, such as a chart, using the answers you give to a series of questions.

Wrapping. A function that causes text to automatically wrap to the next line when it reaches the right edge of a cell.

Workbook. A single Excel file containing a collection of Excel worksheets.

Worksheet. One of several pages in an Excel workbook.

X

X-axis. In a chart, the vertical-value axis.

Y

Y-axis. In a chart, the horizontal-value axis.

Index

Learning Microsoft® Office 2000 is a breeze with PRIMA TECH's bestselling *fast & easy* guides

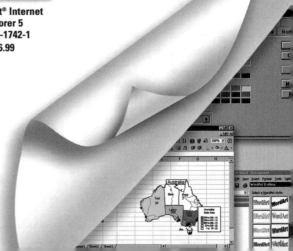